DRAMA CLASSICS

The Drama Classics series aims to offer the world's greatest plays in affordable paperback editions for students, actors and theatregoers. The hallmarks of the series are accessible introductions, uncluttered and uncut texts and an overall theatrical perspective.

Given that readers may be encountering a particular play for the first time, the introduction seeks to fill in the theatrical/historical background and to outline the chief themes rather than concentrate on interpretational and textual analysis. Similarly the play-texts themselves are free of footnotes and other interpolations: instead there is an end-glossary of 'difficult' words and phrases.

The texts of the English-language plays in the series have been prepared taking full account of all existing scholarship. The foreign language plays have been newly translated into a modern English that is both actable and accurate: many of the translators regularly have their work staged professionally.

Under the editorship of Kenneth McLeish, the Drama Classics series is building into a first-class library of dramatic literature representing the best of world theatre.

Series editor: Kenneth McLeish

Associate editors:
Professor Trevor R. Griffiths, *School of Literary and Media Studies, University of North London*

Simon Trussler, *Reader in Drama, Goldsmiths' College, University of London*

Drama Classics   *the first hundred*

The Alchemist
All for Love
Amphitryon
Andromache
Antigone
Arden of Faversham
Bacchae
The Bad-tempered
 Man
The Beaux Stratagem
The Beggar's Opera
Birds
Blood Wedding
Brand
The Broken Jug
The Changeling
The Cherry Orchard
Children of the Sun
El Cid
The Country Wife
Cyrano de Bergerac
The Dance of Death
The Devil is an Ass
Doctor Faustus
A Doll's House
The Duchess of Malfi
Edward II
Electra (Euripides)
Electra (Sophocles)
An Enemy of the People
Enrico IV
The Eunuch
Every Man in his
 Humour
Everyman
The Father
Faust
A Flea in her Ear
Frogs
Fuenteovejuna

The Game of Love and
 Chance
Ghosts
The Government
 Inspector
Hedda Gabler
The Hypochondriac
The Importance of
 Being Earnest
An Italian Straw Hat
The Jew of Malta
King Oedipus
Life is a Dream
The Lower Depths
The Lucky Chance
Lulu
Lysistrata
The Magistrate
The Malcontent
The Man of Mode
The Marriage of
 Figaro
Mary Stuart
The Master Builder
Medea
Menaechmi
The Misanthrope
The Miser
Miss Julie
Molière
A Month in the
 Country
A New Way to Pay
 Old Debts
Oedipus at Kolonos
The Oresteia
Phaedra
Philoctetes
The Playboy of the
 Western World

The Revenger's
 Tragedy
The Rivals
The Robbers
La Ronde
The Rover
The School for
 Scandal
The Seagull
The Servant of Two
 Masters
She Stoops to Conquer
The Shoemaker's
 Holiday
Six Characters in
 Search of an
 Author
Spring's Awakening
Strife
Tartuffe
Thérèse Raquin
Three Sisters
'Tis Pity She's a
 Whore
Too Clever by Half
Ubu
Uncle Vanya
Vassa Zheleznova
Volpone
The Way of the World
The White Devil
The Wild Duck
Women Beware
 Women
Women of Troy
Woyzeck
Yerma

*The publishers welcome
suggestions for further titles*

DRAMA CLASSICS

THE WHITE DEVIL

by
John Webster

with an introduction by
Simon Trussler

NICK HERN BOOKS
London

in association with the

ROYAL SHAKESPEARE COMPANY
Stratford

A Drama Classic

This edition of *The White Devil* first published in Great Britain as a paperback original in 1996 by Nick Hern Books Limited, 14 Larden Road, London W3 7ST

Copyright in the introduction © 1996 Nick Hern Books Limited

The play text is reproduced from the 'Revels Plays' edition of *The White Devil,* published by Manchester University Press, copyright © John Russell Brown 1960 and 1966, by permission. The complete scholarly edition is available from Manchester University Press, Oxford Road, Manchester M13 9NR, UK

Typeset by Country Setting, Woodchurch, Kent TN26 3TB
Printed by BPC, Hazell Books Limited, Aylesbury HP20 1LB

A CIP catalogue record for this book is available from the British Library

ISBN 1 85459 345 5

Introduction

John Webster (*c*. 1580–*c*. 1634)

John Webster came from an evidently prosperous middle-class
London family, his father a coachbuilder and wagonmaker with
premises in Smithfield, just north-west of the City. The business was
continued by John's brother Edward, and perhaps helped to subsidise
Webster's playwriting career – for, by contrast with most professional
dramatists, his output was scarcely sufficient to provide an adequate
living. His law studies in the Middle Temple evidently incomplete,
he is first heard of in the theatre from payments made to Dekker,
Middleton and himself by the manager Philip Henslowe in 1602,
and two years later he was entrusted with the task of fleshing out
Marston's *The Malcontent*, a play written for a children's company,
to meet the needs of the adult players. A number of satirical 'citizen
comedies' of London life, written in collaboration, followed – then,
around 1610, came his first known independent work, *The Devil's
Law Case*, written in the then-fashionable form of a tragi-comedy.
Two or three years later, the two great tragedies which have sustained
his reputation in the theatre followed in quick succession: but whereas
The White Devil received its first performance at the Red Bull, an
open-air theatre of low repute, *The Duchess of Malfi* was performed
by Shakespeare's old company, the King's Men, at their prestigious
indoor house, the Blackfriars – and no doubt also at the second
Globe, where the company still played in the summer months.
Webster's later dramatic output was largely collaborative, with
civic celebrations and occasional verse completing a modest canon.
Beyond these bare facts we know little of his life – or even the exact
date of his death, though his fellow playwright Thomas Heywood
seems to refer to him as dead by 1634.

The White Devil: **What Happens in the Play**

Act One   Count Lodovico, banished from Rome, complains that
worse offenders remain unpunished – notably the Duke Bracciano,
who is openly seducing a married woman, Vittoria Corombona.
Vittoria's brother Flamineo, in the service of Bracciano, learns from
her jealous husband Camillo that he has been denied his wife's
bedchamber. He pretends to urge her to be dutiful to her husband –
but Bracciano finds Vittoria ready to exchange the 'jewel' of her
chastity for the jewel he presents her. She recounts a dream she has
had, which Flamineo interprets as incitement to murder both Camillo
and Bracciano's Duchess, Isabella. Vittoria reacts pleadingly and
Bracciano defiantly to the rebukes of Cornelia, mother to Vittoria
and Flamineo – while Flamineo claims that his own behaviour is
made necessary by the poverty which has been his only inheritance.

Act Two   Isabella discloses to her brother, the Duke Francisco de
Medici, and to Camillo's uncle, the Cardinal Monticelso, her concern
for her husband's fidelity. Alone with the two men, Bracciano is
angered by their protests, but a visit from his sprightly young son
Giovanni seems to persuade him of the need for a reconciliation.
However, he is infuriated by the doting humility of his wife, and
swears on oath that he has divorced her. Monticelso and Francisco
send Camillo in search of Lodovico, in company with Vittoria's
brother Marcello, in order that Bracciano, enabled more openly to
conduct his affair with Vittoria, may be publicly disgraced. By means
of a dumb-show, a conjuror shows Bracciano how, on his orders,
Isabella has been poisoned, and Camillo killed in a pretended
accident, for which Vittoria is to be brought to trial.

Act Three   Flamineo and Marcello argue over Flamineo's role in
Bracciano's affairs, Marcello declaring the 'love of virtue' to be his
own inheritance. The ambassadors arrive to lend authority to the
arraignment of Vittoria, who successfully challenges a Lawyer's
attempt to conduct the proceedings in Latin – the trial thereafter
developing into a duel of words between herself and Monticelso. Cut-
ting short her often dignified though sometimes devious responses,
the Cardinal sentences her, along with her black maidservant Zanche,
to confinement in a house for reformed prostitutes. Flamineo
interprets Bracciano's subsequent reconciliation with Francisco as a
precaution against the discovery of Isabella's death – news of which

is brought by the young Giovanni, in company with the reprieved Lodovico. Flamineo feigns madness to avoid close questioning.

Act Four   Francisco, planning to avenge the death of Isabella, buys the services of Lodovico to advance his cause. He sends a servant with a letter addressed to Vittoria in her confinement, rightly believing that it will be intercepted by Bracciano, who accuses his mistress of being a whore. But, urged on by Flamineo, the two are reconciled, and plot their escape to Padua, there to marry, under cover of the confusion caused by the death of the Pope. The Conclave of Cardinals elect Monticelso as new Pope, and, as Francisco had intended, the excommunication of Vittoria is pronounced: now he plots with Lodovico to take his final revenge against Bracciano – their plans apparently condemned but secretly approved by Monticelso.

Act Five   Disguised as the valiant Moor Mulinassar and two 'noblemen of Hungary', Francisco with Lodovico and Gasparo are welcomed at Bracciano's court. Marcello quarrels with Flamineo over his encouragement of Zanche's affections – but the servant is now attracted to the 'Moor', in whom she promises to confide her secrets. Suddenly, almost casually, Marcello is murdered by Flamineo in front of their mother – but even as Bracciano is condemning him to sue for pardon daily, Lodovico is sprinkling poison into the helmet which the Duke is to wear for the coming tournament. His life despaired of, Bracciano is attended by Lodovico and Gasparo, now disguised as monks, who taunt the demented man with their true identities before strangling him. Flamineo, banished by the new young Duke Giovanni, learns that his mother has been driven mad by the death of Marcello, and finds a 'strange thing . . . compassion' stirring in him. He pretends he had vowed to Bracciano that neither Vittoria nor he should outlive the Duke: but Vittoria and Zanche persuade him to avoid the sin of self-murder by letting them shoot him first, and then taking each other's lives. However, having shot Flamineo, the women trample upon his body – whereupon he reveals that the pistols were not loaded. Lodovico and Gasparo arrive, throw off their disguises, and stab all three, who die lingeringly – Vittoria with a defiance which reconciles Flamineo to his sister. When Giovanni and his party intervene, Lodovico implicates Francisco in the conspiracy before being taken off to the rack and the gallows. Giovanni vows: 'All that have hands in this, shall taste our justice'.

The Spirit of the Jacobean Age

Some writers use the term 'Elizabethan' as if it were synonymous with the 'golden age' of English drama. But this is misleading – for the years of peak theatrical activity, from roughly 1590 to even more roughly 1620, in truth overlapped two reigns. And the coming to the throne of James I in 1603 marked a decisive shift in the national mood – or, more precisely, an acknowledgement of realities which the old Queen had preferred to ignore.

The 1590s had been an uneasy decade, with the war against Spain giving rise to inflation and high taxation as well as diminished trade. Yet the defeat of the Armada in 1588 cast an afterglow over Elizabeth's later years, and her very longevity combined with the charismatic persona she so skilfully projected to conjure an illusion of stability and strength. James's more pacific foreign policy made economic sense: but even in this he alienated his subjects where Elizabeth had wooed them to her ends – and where she had been parsimonious in the national interest, James indulged himself, and was always in need of ready cash. Probably the most satirised of his sources of revenue was the open sale of knighthoods and other honours – and this now seems emblematic of a more pervasive process of commodification: for the forces of capitalist individualism had long been eroding the sense of 'degree, priority and place' which the Tudors had inherited from their medieval forebears.

The influences which shaped Webster's generation were thus quite different from those which helped to form Shakespeare's sensibility only a decade or so earlier. He shared Shakespeare's social class, the lower-middle, but whereas Shakespeare's parents were of the declining rural gentry, Webster's were thrusting urban tradespeople. And while Shakespeare wrote in the shadow of such 'Renaissance men' as Spenser, Sidney, and Marlowe, Webster's contemporaries – the poet Donne, the dramatists Jonson, Middleton, Marston – were of a more pragmatic, even satiric cast of mind, which Webster came to share.

If the tragic heroes of the Elizabethans are typically impelled by overweening ambition towards actions bent on the achievement of knowledge, wealth, or earthly power, Jacobean tragic figures thus tend to be of a less noble, more calculating temper. Sometimes, as in the case of Webster's Flamineo, they are rootless and impoverished hangers-on at court – and the causes of their downfall often spring, as in *The White Devil*, from some unseemly love affair that offends against a social or sexual taboo.

The scandal, intrigue, and violence of Jacobean tragedy has led some moralistic writers to declare it 'decadent': but although the increased technical resources of the indoor playhouses did serve their elite audience's taste for sensationalism, in one sense 'sensationalism' may itself be understood as a concern for *exploring* the human capacity for feeling, through a portrayal of the extremes of emotion and experience. And so, while Hamlet tortures his conscience with intimations of mortality and what might follow, Flamineo is more concerned with the imperatives of living than the fear of death – in which he expects only 'to study a long silence'.

The Jacobean Theatre

A legal obligation to obtain noble patronage was imposed on acting companies in 1572. While this served to reduce the number of strolling 'rogues and vagabonds', as unlicensed actors were called, it gave much greater security to the surviving groups of players – and with security came the confidence to invest in permanent playhouses, of which the first, the Theatre, was built in Shoreditch in 1576.

When James I came to the throne he insisted that these companies should come directly under royal patronage, and the troupe of which Shakespeare was a member, the Lord Chamberlain's, accordingly became the King's Men, while their most notable rivals, the Admiral's, came under the protection of James's eldest son, as Prince Henry's Men. The King's wife, Anne, assumed the patronage of a group of actors previously protected by the Earls of Worcester and Oxford, who now combined to form the Queen's Men – and it was this company, playing at the Red Bull in Clerkenwell, which gave the first performance of *The White Devil* in 1612.

The Red Bull, as its name suggests, was converted from an inn-yard in 1604-5, and was thus similar to other so-called 'public' theatres built in the old Queen's later years – among them the Fortune and the Boar's Head, where Webster's early collaborative efforts of 1603 first reached the stage. In such open-air playhouses, the audiences could stand in an uncovered courtyard which surrounded the raised thrust stage on three sides, or pay extra to sit in one of the tiers of galleries which formed the perimeter of the building – usually polygonal, but probably rectangular in the case of the Red Bull, which was built within the 'square court' of the original inn. This theatre had a reputation for offering boisterous fare to its rowdily inclined spectators – not at all the 'full and understanding' audience for the lack of which, along with bad winter weather, Webster blamed his play's failure in its original performance.

In the professionalised theatre of Jacobean London, Webster was unusual in that he was neither formally attached to a company, like Shakespeare, nor a freelance who made his living from offering his plays to all-comers, like Ben Jonson. He was thus unaccustomed to writing parts to suit particular actors, or plays to please particular audiences – though Richard Perkins, the young actor who first took the role of Flamineo in *The White Devil*, is singled out for praise in Webster's afterword. One suspects that the dramatist preferred the conditions in the Blackfriars theatre, where his other great tragedy, *The Duchess of Malfi*, was first performed in 1613 or 1614.

Such 'private' or indoor theatres had first been used by the occasionally fashionable companies of child actors, but became increasingly popular among the adult professionals after 1609, when the King's Men occupied the Blackfriars as their winter quarters. Here, rows of seats in the 'pit' area of a rectangular auditorium faced an end-on stage, with seating also in the galleries and along the edges of the stage itself. Because the private theatres were more comfortable (and so more expensive) than the open-air houses, and also had a considerably smaller capacity, they are thought to have attracted a socially superior class of audience. But the success of *The Duchess of Malfi* at the Blackfriars – where spectacular stage effects, hard to achieve in the outdoor theatres, were possible – would not have discouraged the King's from keeping the play in their repertoire when they returned to the larger, outdoor Globe during the summer months.

In due course, a later company of Queen's Men is to be found playing *The White Devil* indoors – the second edition of the play, published in 1631, thus claiming that it was 'divers times acted by the Queen's Majesty's Servants, at the Cockpit in Drury Lane'. This theatre (also known, following a fire in 1617, as the Phoenix) probably combined some of the characteristics of the indoor and outdoor houses since, although circular in shape (from the original use its name suggests), it had been roofed over for theatrical performances. The need for artificial lighting would have contributed to creating a claustrophobic, brooding atmosphere for *The White Devil* – while the theatre's smaller size probably also encouraged a more intimate acting style than the Red Bull had expected or allowed.

Finally, it should be remembered that actors at this time were invariably male, as they were to remain until the Restoration in 1660. Some companies employed boys as apprentices to play the younger women such as Vittoria, while adult males would have taken the more mature or 'character' roles such as Cornelia's. This restriction, while perhaps helping to explain the limitations upon the number and the range of women's roles, even in *The White Devil*, none the less makes Webster's creation of so complex and compelling a female character as Vittoria all the more remarkable an achievement.

The Italian Setting and the Play's Source

There were good practical and artistic reasons for the frequency with which Italy provided the setting for Jacobean tragedy. From there in 1520 had come what was widely regarded as a handbook of political intrigue – *The Prince*, by the statesman and philosopher Niccolò Machiavelli (1469-1527), whose very name had (unjustly) become synonymous with devious and plotful statecraft. Still centuries from nation-statehood, Italy was divided between self-governing city-states – most importantly, Milan, Venice, and Florence – and the kingdoms of Naples, Sicily, and Sardinia: and this fragmentation led to constant rivalries and wars, often involving alliances with stronger foreign powers such as France and Spain. All this provided good background settings and raw material for dramatists, while religious themes or references, prohibited in protestant England, could be employed in relation to the displaced Catholic faith – whose centre, of course, was Rome.

The plot of *The White Devil* derived from real-life events in Italy between 1576 and 1585 – so widely reported at the time that it is impossible now to be certain which of the hundred or so documents listed by one commentator provided the dramatist's source. Among those most often cited, and readily accessible to Webster, were the so-called *Fugger Newsletter*, circulated to its clients by the German banking house of that name, and a *Letter Lately Written from Rome* translated into English in 1585.

The historical Vittoria Accoramboni came from an old but impoverished family, and married Francesco Peretti (the original of Camillo), the nephew of the Cardinal Montalto (who becomes Monticelso). Probably in 1580 she met the Duke of Bracciano, whose wife of some twenty years, an actual Isabella, was, however, by then already dead – allegedly murdered by her husband for taking a lover. It was in fact Vittoria's brother Marcello who acted as go-between to his sister and Bracciano, and who assisted in the plot to have the unwanted husband killed. Although the couple then went through a form of marriage, the Pope forbade the match, and Vittoria was confined to a nunnery before being abducted again by her lover.

A crisis seemed to have been precipitated in 1585 when Montalto (like Monticelso) became Pope (as Sixtus V), but this was resolved when Bracciano died, apparently of natural causes, later in the year. The climax to the tragedy actually occurred because neither the powerful Medici family – of whom Isabella's brother Francisco was a member – nor Bracciano's other relatives would accept the will he had made in favour of Vittoria and their child. A real-life Lodovico was indeed involved in the subsequent murders of Vittoria and her younger brother Flamineo, before he himself was strangled in prison. Finally, Marcello was beheaded by order of the Pope in June 1586.

Webster chooses not only to extend the life of his Isabella, but to portray her as an altogether saintlier character than her original. He makes Vittoria and Bracciano more calculating and rather less romantically in love than the sources suggest, while also telescoping the time-scheme of the events. Although he did introduce an entirely unhistorical trial for Vittoria, what may at first sight seem the more 'sensational' ingredients of the play do derive from historical facts – namely Flamineo acting as his sister's pander, and the 'coincidence' of Monticelso's elevation to the papacy at a crucial moment. The total effect is of events seen in a sharper, tighter focus, and of characters who behave less in response to a slow, erratic drift of events than to their own impulsive urges.

Structure and Development

In his prefatory note, 'To the Reader', Webster stresses that in *The White Devil* he has consciously ignored such classical requirements of tragedy as 'height of style, and gravity of person'; nor has he employed a Chorus or *Nuntius* – the messenger of classical drama, who often brought the tidings of some offstage disaster. Neither, for that matter, has he attempted to conform to two of the three neoclassical unities, which would have confined his play to a single setting and a continuous span of time. The resulting freedom of style and 'flow' of action (assisted by the absence of act or scene divisions in the original text) are most probably matters of artistic preference, for which Webster takes the canny precaution of 'blaming' his ill-informed first audience.

The lack of any sub-plot or 'comic relief' does suggest some concern on Webster's part to observe the remaining 'unity', that of action. But while the 'line' of the action is undeviating, any sense of tragic inevitability is subverted by what has been called his 'disjunctive technique', whereby expectations are aroused only to be disappointed, feelings engaged only to be contradicted by their opposite. This technique is itself carefully calculated – its subtleties no doubt contributing to the 'long time . . . finishing this tragedy' to which Webster confesses.

The White Devil may be considered unusual structurally in the apparent brevity of its 'exposition' and 'development' – Lodovico and his friends initially 'setting the scene', the seduction of Vittoria then all but accomplished and the murders planned by the end of the second scene. But this is probably to take an over-psychologised approach to a play which appears to be less concerned with an illicit love which sweeps aside all barriers than with the causes for revenge its relentless pursuit sets in motion.

The 'Arraignment of Vittoria' is in this sense central alike to the play's thematic and chronological development – a development which is essentially 'dialectical', each stage of the action inviting a certain response, which in turn changes the nature of the situation, and so invites a modification of that response. Our attitude to the main characters is kept in such a constant state of flux that their deaths become the 'resolution' not just of the play but of our own (perhaps unconscious) debate about their natures: tragic 'inevitability' is thus at once complicated yet curiously heightened by the unexpectedness of events and the sheer cussedness of human behaviour.

The Language of the Play

In the late 1580s, the dramatist Christopher Marlowe made 'blank verse' the distinctive vehicle for Elizabethan tragedy – unrhymed lines of ten syllables, divided into five feet, with the stress generally falling on the second syllable of each. By the turn of the new century Shakespeare and his contemporaries had developed the idiom into a highly flexible instrument – by the use of lines which were not 'end-stopped', by changes in the expected pattern of stress, by subtle manipulation of the 'caesura' (the 'felt pause' modulating each line), by deliberate metric irregularities for emphatic purposes – and through a variety of other devices intended to fit the verse to the constantly changing dramatic needs of a play. Rhyme was in the main reserved for climactic effects, to indicate the closing lines of set speeches, as a 'tag' for the ending of a scene – or, as often in Webster, to suggest the rhetorical quotation-marks of a 'sententious' moral.

Generally, neoclassical 'decorum' required prose to be employed for characters of lowly status, or when a comic or down-to-earth tone was required. In *The White Devil* the speech of Flamineo is a particularly interesting mixture of verse and prose – verse generally being employed for the more formal, courtly, or introspective dialogue, prose when he appears in more anecdotal, casual, or impromptu vein. Since there are no 'low-life' scenes or comic interludes in this play, none of its major characters speaks only in prose, but Webster's use of blank verse, though it sometimes appears almost slapdash, in fact creates a highly varied effect both in the tonal colouring it can achieve, and as 'punctuation' to the rhetorical development of a speech.

The director John Barton has summed up Shakespeare's blank verse as 'stage directions in shorthand': and in some ways this description applies even more pertinently to Webster's. In *The White Devil*, he uses blank verse both as a highly formal medium – as in Monticelso's 'Shall I expound whore to you?' speech (III, ii, 78-101) – and also in an almost naturalistic fashion, as in the cut-and-thrust of argument between Vittoria and her accuser, which is further broken up by interjections from Francisco and reflections from the ambassadors (III, ii, 101-24). Even in this short episode the effects are many and various: for example, two or three characters may share the same metric line (104, 109-10), or the addition of an extra syllable (known as a 'feminine ending') may assist the continuity of sense into the next line (108) or give added emphasis (121), while Webster's tendency to alternate short, sharp sentences, colloquial rather than grammatical, with more formal speech effectively sharpens the attention we pay to both (110-18).

It is useful to consider how, in performance, the frequent need for lines to 'run on' induces a creative tension between the metrical impulse to pause and the natural continuity of the meaning; how the stresses suggested by the sense and by the rhetorical weight can work fruitfully against the expected rhythm of the metre; and how the continuity of broken lines shared metrically between two or more speakers can create a quite different sense of timing and energy from end-stopped dialogue.

With its abrupt metrical variations and a flow of thought that can appear disjointed, Webster's verse often traces what we would today call a character's 'stream of consciousness' – its impact nicely summed up by the critic Muriel Bradbrook as 'small packets of energy' which are 'implosive rather than explosive'. The reader, especially, needs also to consider when and how the verse structure calls for a beat or more of silence – whether to accommodate uncertainty, reflection, or simply some necessary stage business.

The Elizabethan and Jacobean ages were of immense importance in shaping the English language we know today, both in terms of the enrichment of its vocabulary and of the gradual 'fixing' of grammar and syntax as the spread of printing slowed down the process of steady change through spoken usage. Sometimes we may not even be aware of the significance of what to us seems simply an archaic form, but which Webster is using purposefully. For example, in II, ii, the respectful (and now universal) usage 'your' sometimes gives way to the now discarded 'thy', which was normally reserved for more intimate exchanges, for talking to social inferiors, or (as on occasion here) dismissively, in moments of angry tension.

Verbal Imagery and Visual Spectacle

In studying any great play from the past, it is often difficult to separate out the qualities which make it timeless from those which make it (perhaps no less valuably) a product of its own time. It is equally so with the criticism written about such plays, which may in one period be almost exclusively concerned with 'moral' values, in another with the way in which 'character' is presented, or in another with the way in which the language of the writer reflects his supposed concerns.

Partly in reaction to the naturalistically-derived, 'biographical' approach to Shakespeare of commentators like A. C. Bradley, the critic Caroline Spurgeon in her book *Shakespeare's Imagery* (1935) proved influential in encouraging many later writers to examine other Elizabethan and Jacobean dramatists through their use of 'imagery' – which may most simply be defined either as the drawing of word-pictures which relate to the action in an illustrative way, or as the recurrent use of a particular kind of vocabulary (medical, legal, horticultural, or whatever) which, consciously or unconsciously, colours our impression of the accompanying action.

In Act V of *The White Devil* alone, Muriel Bradbrook tells us, are clustered some 30 references to animals – notably the wolf and the dog. And Ralph Berry reckons that 66 images out of a total of about 500 in the play (some 13 per cent) are concerned with disease or corruption. We can take note of these as we read, and may be similarly alert to the number of references to jewels and glass, or to painting – or to blood, in a wide spectrum of meanings, from life itself, to a sense of family ties, to sexual passion.

Such tracing of strands of verbal imagery can be quite a rewarding exercise for the reader – not least because we need to look closely at the text in a way that goes beyond wondering 'what happens next': but this should be in recognition that the experience of the play in the theatre seldom encourages such image-spotting – and, when it does, usually counterposes a visual dimension. Thus, of the strands of imagery already mentioned, that of corruption of the flesh is vividly brought to life when the ghost of Bracciano produces a skull from beneath the lily flowers (V, iv, 124-41); while painting is instrumental in a literal rather than a figurative sense in the murder of Isabella, as 'portrayed' in dumb-show (II, ii).

Such visual elements, creating what are virtually 'set-pieces' of dramatic spectacle, have sometimes been dubbed gratuitously sensational. Yet while, say, the dumb-shows evoked by the Conjuror (II, ii) at one level simply induce a supernatural thrill, they also serve intellectually to 'distance' the murders of Isabella and Camillo (giving them a quite different quality from the murders of the final act), and to focus our attention on the response of Bracciano to these events. Similarly, the ghost of Isabella (IV, i) not only carries a shock value, but 'embodies' a significance inseparable from the conventions of the revenge tradition – serving, like the Ghost of Hamlet's Father, to quicken the avenger's purpose.

Lesser instances abound, and can be mutually illuminating. There is spectacle alike in the horrible parody of extreme unction which attends Bracciano's death (V, iii, 130-78), and in the pathetic trappings which surround Marcello's (V, iv, 66-111) – while their close juxtaposition carries an implicit, ironic comment on the contrast between the deaths of a rich duke and an impoverished follower.

The 'Arraignment of Vittoria' (III, ii) offers spectacle of a more formal kind, as do the ceremonies surrounding the election of the new Pope (IV, iii) or the preparations for the tournament intended to celebrate Bracciano's marriage (V, ii-iii). In each of these cases, the circumstances are steeped in symbolic associations carried over from their real-life equivalents, while at the same time conveying the added significance of their relation to the events of the play and the attitudes of the characters towards what they are 'performing', which we may further contrast with their attitudes in less 'public' circumstances.

Characterisation

In considering 'characterisation' in a play of this period, we need to bear in mind that the psychological analysis of human behaviour on a 'scientific' basis has its beginnings only in the nineteenth century, and that 'character' in the seventeenth century was more usually defined in relation to moral characteristics or to 'types'. 'Character writing' in this sense became a popular English prose form following the appearance of a translation into Latin of the *Characteroi* of the

Greek writer Theophrastus in 1592, and collections of English 'characters' were put together by Bishop Hall in 1608, by Sir Thomas Overbury in 1614, and by John Earle in 1628.

In works of this kind, characters were presented either as the personifications of universal vices and virtues, or as exemplifying a particular social or political type of the day – rather as Monticelso expounds the 'perfect character' of a whore (III, ii, 78-101). This approach to characterisation is also evident in, for example, the 'comedies of humours' written by Webster's contemporary Ben Jonson, with their delineation of individuals ruled by a predominant passion, such as greed, lust or ambition.

Webster himself contributed some new essays to the sixth edition of Overbury's *Characters* in 1615 – among them a sketch of 'An Excellent Actor', identified as being a 'grave orator' able to display Nature as she is, 'neither on stilts nor crutches', and as one who 'fortifies moral precepts with examples'. As this suggests, we should not expect simply or fully to 'understand' the characters of *The White Devil* in psychological terms – and still less should we use 'probability' as a yardstick by which to judge them, or try to create 'imaginary biographies' of their pasts, as some actors do for characters in modern realistic plays.

As Webster's own concern with 'nature' suggests, this is not to imply that the play lacks psychological depth: but such depth is displayed as much in how the characters act as in how they interact, more in terms of 'what they do' than of 'how they think'. Thus, there are reasons or 'motives' to be found for Flamineo's actions: but it is probably more helpful to understand him through his behaviour and his own attempts at a kind of self-definition: he *becomes* what he does and what he says.

Webster's Jacobean view of character types can be traced back to Aristotle's urging of the pre-eminence in a play of action over character. Thus, in the *Poetics*, a man's happiness or otherwise is said to be decided by the choices he makes – especially 'when those are not obvious'. And this comes close to a definition of what we would today call 'existential' choice, after the philosophical view that 'existence precedes essence' – the belief that our individuality is shaped not (as the realists held) through the deterministic effects of heredity and environment, but, as with the characters of *The White Devil*, existentially, through the sum of our actions and our making of meaningful choices.

And so, while Flamineo clearly embodies the distinctive Jacobean character type of the malcontent, as does Francisco that of the revenger, both transcend their typology through their actions – and it is part of the play's dialectic challenge that we are left to decide for ourselves whether those actions have fulfilled or disappointed the search for self-definition which supersedes the immediacy of declared motives.

The Revenge Tradition

One of the main classical influences on English dramatists was the work of Seneca, a Roman writer from the early Christian era. His plays were full of violence and bloodshed, and his imitators among the Elizabethan and Jacobean dramatists shed their own characters' blood as often as not in the pursuit of revenge. This was not only a recurrent but a topical theme in an age when the conflict between the pursuit of personal and social justice remained unresolved.

One of the first and most popular of the 'revenge tragedies' inspired by Seneca was Thomas Kyd's *The Spanish Tragedy*, written *c.* 1589. Marston's *Antonio's Revenge* (1599), Chapman's *Revenge of Bussy D'Ambois* (1610), and the archetypally-named *The Revenger's Tragedy* (1607) were other popular examples of the form. *The White Devil* duly shares with *The Revenger's Tragedy* such characteristics as a setting in an Italian court, a bunch of unscrupulous nobles, underlings ruled by appetite rather than duty, a duke illicitly in love, a melancholic of reduced fortunes, skulls, gruesome poisonings – and, in the end, various other forms of grotesque carnage.

But in *The Revenger's Tragedy* the protagonist is clearly Vendice, who avenges the murder of his betrothed after she has refused the advances of an evil duke – whereas it would be difficult to claim that Webster's avenger, Francisco, is truly the protagonist, let alone the 'hero' of *The White Devil*. Here, revenge has become not the noble redemption of personal or family honour, but a scurrilous business eventually carried out at second-hand by hired assassins. The Machiavellian Francisco is even left alive and in apparent safety at the end of the play, as is his erstwhile fellow-conspirator Monticelso – though the young Duke Giovanni's climactic call for 'justice' amounts, in effect, to a threat of perpetuated revenge.

While Webster was well aware of the conventions of 'revenge tragedy' and of the audience expectations aroused by the form, he none the less reshaped it to his own ironic ends. Flamineo is like Hamlet in assuming the guise of the melancholic – yet so far from being the revenger, he is instrumental in precipitating the need for revenge. The original murders of Isabella and Camillo are committed not to further lust or ambition, but to *prevent* the revenge of the wronged wife and husband so graphically anticipated in Vittoria's dream (I, ii, 229-55). And a final irony is that Bracciano's murder is, like Isabella's, by means of a poison which touches his lips – although the means are chosen before Francisco has learned from Zanche the nature of his sister's death.

For an evil schemer akin to Flamineo in the Shakespearean canon we have to look to *Othello* – in which Iago is interesting precisely because of his *lack* of motives. Yet while Iago is no more concerned with money than most characters in Shakespeare's plays, there is a strong economic imperative to Flamineo's actions, as is made acrimoniously explicit in the argument with his mother over his lack of an inheritance (I, ii, 308-45).

The first, false death of Flamineo actually parodies the kind of dying speeches to which revenge heroes were prone (V, vi, 100-44) – and, played with style, it may permissibly become quite funny, since an audience should only be deceived if Webster (and Flamineo) are assumed to be capable of intending such lines as 'My liver's parboiled like Scotch holy-bread' to be taken seriously. The scene leaves us not only prepared to accept the ensuing, actual deaths temporarily purged of the dangerous inclination to laugh at their sheer quantity, but questioning further the nature of the 'reality' of the dying rhetoric that has so recently been mocked. What might at first have seemed just another variation upon an over-used formula thus becomes, at one of the play's many levels of meaning, a wry commentary upon the causes, nature and consequences of revenge itself.

The Church, the Social Order, and the Family

When *The White Devil* was first performed, the English Reformation carried through by Henry VIII was less than a century old. Indeed, the Elizabethan settlement, its defining form, preceded Webster's birth by only a few decades, and the religious justification claimed by Spain for restoring the Catholic faith in England remained inextricably linked with the political and military struggles which continued through his childhood and formative years. In other parts of Europe the issue remained yet more finely balanced – as recently as 1572, just before the real-life events on which *The White Devil* was based, tens of thousands of Protestants having died in France during and after the Massacre of St. Bartholomew's Day. This slaughter took place on the orders of the King's mother, Catherine de Medici – a member of that powerful Italian family from which come the originals of Isabella and Francisco in Webster's play.

Although the Catholic Church had already taken measures to curb the worst corruptions within its ranks, it remained associated with such powerful political interests – not least in Italy itself, where the Pope was political as well as spiritual head of the Papal States spread around the City of Rome. Here the Church maintained its own administrative bureaucracy, largely under the control of that College of Cardinals of which Monticelso, like his real-life original, is a leading member – one of whose functions was (as in the play, and as it remains) to take responsibility for electing a new Pope.

The cardinals themselves constituted the highest rank in a hierarchy which stretched down to the humblest parish priest, and which mirrored the gradations of social life outside the Church. Francisco, as Duke of Florence, and Monticelso thus meet on a roughly equal footing – hence, perhaps, the slight ambivalence of Francisco, in acknowledging but not entirely endorsing the judgement of the ecclesiastical court before which Vittoria is arraigned.

The threat of excommunication, which Monticelso exerts over Bracciano and Vittoria, was also used by the Church to try to bring into line recalcitrant political leaders. But Bracciano becomes very much his own person once he is restored to his own territory, and – as Francisco acknowledges in his reluctance to settle his quarrel by armed conflict (IV, i, 1-14) – in practice the authority of the Church could only be enforced through sometimes uncomfortable political and dynastic connections. Despite the precariousness of the reconciliations between Francisco and Bracciano after Isabella's 'divorce' and again after the condemnation of Vittoria, these suggest how piety had often to give way before political expediency. However, since churchmen could not marry, their power could not be perpetuated through dynastic inheritance, as it was in such great secular families as the Medici – although such families could consolidate their strength by occupying high positions in the Church, and two of the Medici line actually rose to become Popes.

The plight of Flamineo is that he has inherited no means to keep up the honourable name of his own, less well-connected family – of which, as the eldest son of a dead father, he is now the head. For all the pragmatism of his morality, he recognises some residual family loyalty in accepting that his mother and brother should join the party for Padua. And, significantly, it is only when, as Bracciano's brother-in-law, he becomes part of his family, that he briefly feels his happiness to be assured.

Francisco seems to have little real affection for his sister Isabella, and Monticelso ill disguises his contempt for his nephew Camillo: both act against Bracciano's betrayal of their relatives not from feelings of love, but to preserve their family's honour. And whether or not Bracciano and Vittoria marry for love, such a motive evidently had little influence over their earlier choices – Bracciano having taken Isabella to achieve a prudent dynastic alliance with the Medici, and Vittoria marrying Camillo for his money, inadequate though she claims this to have been.

Justice, Reward, and the Sense of Self

For a play which gives an irresistible impression of a world in moral disorder, *The White Devil* is much concerned with matters of justice – punishment for sin, rewards for services rendered. Lodovico in the opening scene has been punished, apparently justly, and in one of those 'short syllables / That stand for periods' so characteristic of the play, his terse exclamation 'Courtly reward! / And Punishment!' has been taken by some critics to sum up its dominant theme.

Certainly, Vittoria is wooed not with professions of love but promises of reward – from a jewel in exchange for the 'jewel' of her chastity to the ultimate reward of becoming Bracciano's duchess. Even the election of the Pope is hedged about with hints of corruption (IV, iii, 24-32), while Lodovico is quite prepared to believe the elevated Monticelso capable of secret bribery – 'the modest form of greatness!' (IV, iii, 143). And the final act is bursting with references to rewards and, of course, to punishments: it is here that Flamineo, claiming from Vittoria a 'Reward, for my long service', is allotted instead the portion of Cain for the murder of his brother.

Taken in connection with the large number of references also to 'princes', 'politicians', and 'great men' – the dispensers of earthly rewards and punishments – this preoccupation with rewards sheds an ironic light on Webster's single direct quotation from that supposed exemplar of Italianate villainy, Machiavelli. It is, aptly enough, spoken by Francisco's hireling, Gasparo:

> Fool! Princes give rewards with their own hands
> But death or punishment by the hands of others. (V, vi, 185-6)

Political theory also had it that in dispensing justice human princes were acting on behalf of the divine will – a role the child Giovanni is said to be fulfilling at the end of the play.

In that orthodoxly Christian sense, dependence upon earthly rewards is in any case futile – yet the play itself suggests that any hope of reward beyond this life is similarly doomed. Thus, the virtuous Marcello is denied even a Christian burial – and earlier has seemed to accept that he is condemned by association (V, ii, 20-2). Bracciano is denied the Church's last rites, and so the chance of redemption – Francisco and Lodovico also being damned for so denying him. And Vittoria and Flamineo both die unrepentant and unredeemed, Vittoria's last words more a reflection on the deceptive nature of princely rewards than an anticipation of heavenly judgement:

> O happy they that never saw the court,
> Nor ever knew great man but by report. (V, vi, 261-2)

If Webster has, indeed, chosen to distribute a concern with rewards and their dispensation among so many of his characters as a way of organising his thoughts, an audience receives this concern primarily as an aspect of characterisation. In the theatre it is very difficult to 'receive' (let alone to convey) the Christian 'message' that some critics have read into the play – that judgement is ultimately in the hands of God. Other critics suggest that the profession of a faith in one's self rather than in God is something that most characters in the play seem to share – and which is summed up in Lodovico's cry as he is dragged off to the rack and the gallows:

> I do glory yet,
> That I can call this act mine own. (V, vi, 293-4)

If Webster's is not a godless world, it is thus one in which the dying characters seem, like Flamineo, to be 'i' th' way to study a long silence' (V, vi, 203).

'The Skull beneath the Skin'

In his poem 'Whispers of Immortality', T.S. Eliot, himself much influenced by Webster's work, wrote

> Webster was much possessed by death
> And saw the skull beneath the skin,
> And breastless creatures underground
> Leaned backwards with a lipless grin.

The macabre image is as striking as one of Webster's own – and another poet, Rupert Brooke, conjured up a similar picture in his judgement that a 'play of Webster's is full of the feverish and ghastly turmoil of a nest of maggots'. However, *The White Devil* is not about corpses, but characters with as strong a sense of life as of death, whose 'feverish and ghastly turmoil', unlike that of a nest of maggots, must make dramatic if not wholly rational sense.

Is Webster's a godless universe? Certainly, there are plentiful references to devils in the action as well as in the title of *The White Devil* – and Vittoria herself, the presumed 'white devil', is also referred to as 'the devil in crystal' (IV, ii, 88). But the reference is to a colloquial saying rather than some abstruse theological paradox, and none of the devils called up so casually in the play seems to be engaged in combat with God, whatever their intentions towards man. They are mentioned without any real scriptural or theological precision, and indeed seem closer in spirit to the minor vices and devils of the old morality plays – sometimes even becoming, like those impish vices, perversely sympathetic, as when Flamineo approvingly refers to Vittoria as an 'excellent devil' early in the play (I, ii, 256).

Webster's devils, then, function primarily in relation to a dramatic action. If the characters in this action are more complex than the personified virtues and vices of the moralities, they are, even so, no more and no less than the sum of the attributes Webster gives them, and they operate within the confines of certain stage conventions, however stretched by the dramatist to suit his own purposes.

We may, perhaps, legitimately expect that it is within the nature of a tragedy in some way to help us reconcile ourselves to the imminence of mortality, the inescapable fact of death. With that expectation, to suggest that Webster's characters accommodate the knowledge of death within the process of their living is not to say that the play is nihilistic. Rather, it is to suggest that they take a total responsibility for their actions, and finally accept the consequences of those actions, in a way that makes them different in kind from the protagonists of Shakespeare's tragedies, who find themselves caught up in an inexorable process of self-discovery.

Webster's characters don't 'develop' in that sense, and it is at least arguable that they are more rather than less 'realistic' in this, if typicality is to some degree a measure of dramatic realism – for human 'development' is not usually so decisive, or even so clearly discernible, as Macbeth's or King Lear's. If Shakespeare's tragedy is, more classically, the tragedy of men of essentially noble stature who undergo a change, whether of fortune or of self, Webster's characters are probably closer to the muddled, selfish, intractable people most of us encounter most of the time.

A Note on the Text

Our text of *The White Devil* is based upon that of the first edition (or 'first quarto') of 1612, which appeared in the year of the play's earliest performance, and is thought to have been typeset from a manuscript prepared by Webster for the printer, not, as often happened, from a script used by the actors. Even so, it contains relatively few stage directions – and no act or scene divisions. Those used in our edition were first proposed by the textual scholar W. W. Greg, and have been retained for convenience in most modern editions of *The White Devil:* but it should be stressed that they have no authority, and that their original absence is not a matter of care-lessness, but a reflection of the continuous flow of action in the Elizabethan and Jacobean open-air theatres.

Simon Trussler

Webster: Key Dates

1580	*c*. Born, probably in London. Almost certainly attended Merchant Taylors' School, in the City of London.
1597	Probably became a law student in the Middle Temple.
1602	Payments recorded to Webster for work on three lost plays.
1604	Wrote the Induction (introductory scene) to Marston's tragi-comedy *The Malcontent*, and collaborated with Dekker on the comedy of city life *Westward Ho!*
1605	Collaborated with Dekker on a second 'city comedy', *Northward Ho!* Marriage to Sara, who bore him several children after 1606, around this time.
1608	Probable first performance of *Appius and Virginia*, written with Thomas Heywood (but dated by some critics as late as 1622).
1610	First performance of his earliest known independent work, *The Devil's Law Case* (alternatively ascribed to 1617).
1612	First performance of *The White Devil*, at the Red Bull, poorly received. Contributed verses to Heywood's *Apology for Actors*.
1614	Probable first performance of *The Duchess of Malfi*.
1615	Contributions to a new edition of Overbury's *Characters*.
1617	Probable date of his lost play, *Guise*, reputedly a comedy.
1620	Possibly collaborated with Middleton on the comedy *Anything for a Quiet Life*.
1624	Collaborated with Dekker, Ford, and Rowley on the lost topical tragedy *The Late Murder of the Son upon the Mother*.
1625	Collaboration with Heywood and Rowley on the comedy *A Cure for a Cuckold*.
1634	Referred to as dead in Heywood's *Hierarchy of the Blessed Angels*.

For Further Reading

For more advanced study of *The White Devil*, the editions of Elizabeth M. Brennan in the 'New Mermaids' series (London: Benn) and of John Russell Brown in the 'Revels Plays' series (Manchester University Press) are recommended. *Three Plays*, edited by D.C. Gunby for the 'Penguin Classics' series, provides a convenient collection which also includes *The Duchess of Malfi* and *The Devil's Law-Case*.

The closest we have to a biography of this elusive dramatist is M.C. Bradbrook's *John Webster: Citizen and Dramatist* (London: Weidenfeld, 1980). G.K. and S.K. Hunter have edited a useful volume on Webster in the 'Penguin Critical Anthologies' series (Harmondsworth, 1969), and a further selection is offered in the 'Mermaid Critical Anthologies' series, edited by B. Morris (London, 1970). D.B. Moore's *Webster: the Critical Heritage* (London: Routledge, 1981) traces the course of earlier critical opinion.

Helpful studies of *The White Devil* include D.C. Gunby's in the 'Studies in English Literature' series (London: Arnold, 1971), and J.R. Mulryne's article, '*The White Devil* and *The Duchess of Malfi*', in *Jacobean Theatre*, edited by J.R. Brown and B. Harris (London: Arnold, 1960). This volume also remains useful for background reading, but *The Cambridge Companion to English Renaissance Drama*, edited by A. R. Braunmuller and Michael Hattaway (Cambridge, 1990), now offers a wider-ranging account of the social and theatrical contexts, as well as helpful guides to further reading. M.C. Bradbrook's *Themes and Conventions of Elizabethan Tragedy* (Cambridge, 1935) was a pioneering generic study, while for a full overview of the theatrical conditions Andrew Gurr's *The Shakespearian Stage, 1574-1642* (Cambridge, 1970) has not been bettered.

To the Reader

In publishing this tragedy, I do but challenge to myself that liberty, which other men have ta'en before me; not that I affect praise by it, for, *nos haec novimus esse nihil*, only since it was acted, in so dull a time of winter, presented in so open and black a theatre, that it wanted (that which is the only grace and setting out of a tragedy) a full and understanding auditory: and that since that time I have noted, most of the people that come to that playhouse, resemble those ignorant asses (who visiting stationers' shops their use is not to inquire for good books, but new books) I present it to the general view with this confidence:

Nec rhoncos metues, maligniorum,
Nec scombris tunicas, dabis molestas.

If it be objected this is no true dramatic poem, I shall easily confess it, – *non potes in nugas dicere plura meas: ipse ego quam dixi,*—willingly, and not ignorantly, in this kind have I faulted: for should a man present to such an auditory, the most sententious tragedy that ever was written, observing all the critical laws, as height of style, and gravity of person, enrich it with the sententious *Chorus*, and as it were lifen death, in the passionate and weighty *Nuntius:* yet after all this divine rapture, *O dura messorum ilia*, the breath that comes from the uncapable multitude is able to poison it, and ere it be acted, let the author resolve to fix to every scene, this of Horace,

Haec hodie porcis comedenda relinques.

To those who report I was a long time in finishing this tragedy, I confess I do not write with a goose-quill, winged with two feathers, and if they will needs make it my fault, I must answer them with that of Euripides to Alcestides, a tragic writer: Alcestides objecting that Euripides had only in three days composed three verses, whereas himself had written three hundred: 'Thou tell'st truth,' (quoth he) 'but here's the difference, – thine shall only be read for three days, whereas mine shall continue three ages.'

Detraction is the sworn friend to ignorance: for mine own part I have ever truly cherish'd my good opinion of other men's worthy labours, especially of that full and height'ned style of Master Chapman, the labour'd and understanding works of Master Jonson: the no less worthy composures of the both worthily excellent Master Beaumont, and Master Fletcher: and lastly (without wrong last to be named) the right happy and copious industry of Master Shakespeare, Master Dekker, and Master Heywood, wishing what I write may be read by their light: protesting, that, in the strength of mine own judgement, I know them so worthy, that though I rest silent in my own work, yet to most of theirs I dare (without flattery) fix that of Martial:

non norunt, hæc monumenta mori.

THE WHITE DEVIL

Dramatis Personae

MONTICELSO, *a Cardinal, later Pope* PAUL IV.

FRANCISCO *de* MEDICI, *Duke of Florence; in the last Act, disguised as*
    MULINASSAR, *a Moor.*

The Duke of BRACCIANO, *otherwise, Paulo Giordano Orsini; husband first*
    of Isabella, and later of Vittoria.

GIOVANNI, *his son by Isabella.*

Count LODOVICO, *sometimes known as Lodowick; in love with Isabella;*
    later a conspirator in the pay of Francisco.

CAMILLO, *first husband of Vittoria, cousin to Monticelso.*

ANTONELLI,

GASPARO, *friends to Lodovico; later conspirators in the pay of Francisco.*

CARLO,

PEDRO, *of Bracciano's household; in secret league with Francisco.*

HORTENSIO, *of Bracciano's household.*

FLAMINEO, *secretary to Bracciano; brother to Vittoria.*

MARCELLO, *his younger brother; of Francisco's household.*

ARRAGON, *a Cardinal.*

JULIO, *a doctor.*

ISABELLA, *first wife of Bracciano; sister to Francisco.*

VITTORIA COROMBONA, a *Venetian lady; wife first of Camillo, and*
    later of Bracciano.

CORNELIA, *mother to Vittoria, Marcello, and Flamineo.*

ZANCHE, *a Moor; servant to Vittoria; in love first with Flamineo, and later*
    with Francisco.

Ambassadors; Courtiers; Officers and Guards; Attendants.

Conjuror; Chancellor, Register and Lawyers; Conclavist; Armourer;
    Physicians; Page.

Matron of the House of Convertites; Ladies.

Scene: Rome for the first four acts, Padua for the fifth.

Act One, Scene One

Enter Count LODOVICO, ANTONELLI *and* GASPARO.

LODOVICO. Banish'd?

ANTONELLI.   It griev'd me much to hear the sentence.

LODOVICO. Ha, ha, O Democritus thy gods
    That govern the whole world! – Courtly reward,
    And punishment! Fortune's a right whore.
    If she give aught, she deals it in small parcels,   5
    That she may take away all at one swoop.
    This 'tis to have great enemies, God quite them:
    Your wolf no longer seems to be a wolf
    Than when she's hungry.

GASPARO.   You term those enemies
    Are men of princely rank.

LODOVICO.   O I pray for them.   10
    The violent thunder is adored by those
    Are pash'd in pieces by it.

ANTONELLI.   Come my lord,
    You are justly doom'd; look but a little back
    Into your former life: you have in three years
    Ruin'd the noblest earldom –

GASPARO.   Your followers   15
    Have swallowed you like mummia, and being sick
    With such unnatural and horrid physic
    Vomit you up i' th' kennel –

ANTONELLI.   All the damnable degrees
    Of drinkings have you stagger'd through – one citizen
    Is lord of two fair manors, call'd you master   20
    Only for caviare.

GASPARO.   Those noblemen
   Which were invited to your prodigal feasts,
   Wherein the phoenix scarce could scape your throats,
   Laugh at your misery, as fore-deeming you
   An idle meteor which drawn forth the earth   25
   Would be soon lost i' th' air.

ANTONELLI.   Jest upon you,
   And say you were begotten in an earthquake,
   You have ruin'd such fair lordships.

LODOVICO.   Very good, –
   This well goes with two buckets, I must tend
   The pouring out of either.

GASPARO.   Worse than these,   30
   You have acted certain murders here in Rome,
   Bloody and full of horror.

LODOVICO.   'Las they were flea-bitings:
   Why took they not my head then?

GASPARO.   O my lord
   The law doth sometimes mediate, thinks it good
   Not ever to steep violent sins in blood, –   35
   This gentle penance may both end your crimes,
   And in the example better these bad times.

LODOVICO. So, – but I wonder then some great men scape
   This banishment, – there's Paulo Giordano Orsini,
   The Duke of Bracciano, now lives in Rome,   40
   And by close pandarism seeks to prostitute
   The honour of Vittoria Corombona, –
   Vittoria, she that might have got my pardon
   For one kiss to the duke.

ANTONELLI. Have a full man within you, –   45
   We see that trees bear no such pleasant fruit
   There where they grew first, as where they are new set.
   Perfumes the more they are chaf'd the more they render
   Their pleasing scents, and so affliction
   Expresseth virtue, fully, whether true,   50
   Or else adulterate.

LODOVICO.   Leave your painted comforts, –
   I'll make Italian cut-works in their guts
   If ever I return.

GASPARO.   O sir.

LODOVICO.   I am patient, –
   I have seen some ready to be executed
   Give pleasant looks, and money, and grown familiar   55
   With the knave hangman, so do I, – I thank them,
   And would account them nobly merciful
   Would they dispatch me quickly, –

ANTONELLI.   Fare you well,
   We shall find time I doubt not to repeal
   Your banishment.

LODOVICO.   I am ever bound to you: 60

A sennet sounds.

This is the world's alms; – pray make use of it, –
   Great men sell sheep, thus to be cut in pieces,
   When first they have shorn them bare and sold their fleeces.

Exeunt.

Act One, Scene Two

Enter BRACCIANO, CAMILLO, FLAMINEO, VITTORIA
COROMBONA [, *and* ATTENDANTS].

BRACCIANO. Your best of rest.

VITTORIA.   Unto my lord the duke,
   The best of welcome. More lights, attend the duke.

   [*Exeunt* CAMILLO *and* VITTORIA.]

BRACCIANO. Flamineo.

FLAMINEO.   My lord.

BRACCIANO.   Quite lost Flamineo.

FLAMINEO. Pursue your noble wishes, I am prompt
    As lightning to your service, – O my lord!   5
    (*Whispers.*) The fair Vittoria, my happy sister
    Shall give you present audience, – gentlemen
    Let the caroche go on, and 'tis his pleasure
    You put out all your torches and depart.

    [*Exeunt* ATTENDANTS.]

BRACCIANO. Are we so happy?

FLAMINEO.   Can 't be otherwise?   10
    Observ'd you not tonight my honour'd lord
    Which way soe'er you went she threw her eyes?
    I have dealt already with her chamber-maid
    Zanche the Moor, and she is wondrous proud
    To be the agent for so high a spirit.   15

BRACCIANO. We are happy above thought, because 'bove merit.

FLAMINEO. 'Bove merit! we may now talk freely: 'bove merit;
    what is 't you doubt? her coyness? that's but the superficies
    of lust most women have; yet why should ladies blush to
    hear that nam'd, which they do not fear to handle? O they   20
    are politic, they know our desire is increas'd by the difficulty
    of enjoying; whereas satiety is a blunt, weary and drowsy
    passion, – if the buttery-hatch at court stood continually open
    there would be nothing so passionate crowding, nor hot suit
    after the beverage, –   25

BRACCIANO. O but her jealous husband.

FLAMINEO. Hang him, a gilder that hath his brains perish'd
    with quick-silver is not more cold in the liver. The great bar-
    riers moulted not more feathers than he hath shed hairs,
    by the confession of his doctor. An Irish gamester that   30
    will play himself naked, and then wage all downward, at
    hazard, is not more venturous. So unable to please a
    woman that like a Dutch doublet all his back is shrunk
    into his breeches.

    Shroud you within this closet, good my lord, –   35
    Some trick now must be thought on to divide

My brother-in-law from his fair bed-fellow, –

BRACCIANO. O should she fail to come, –

FLAMINEO. I must not have your lordship thus unwisely
  amorous, – I myself have loved a lady and pursued her with   40
  a great deal of under-age protestation, whom some three or
  four gallants that have enjoyed would with all their hearts
  have been glad to have been rid of: 'tis just like a summer
  birdcage in a garden, – the birds that are without, despair
  to get in, and the birds that are within despair and are in a   45
  consumption for fear they shall never get out: away away
  my lord, –

  [*Exit* BRACCIANO]. *Enter* CAMILLO.

  [*Aside.*] See here he comes, this fellow by his apparel
  Some men would judge a politician,
  But call his wit in question you shall find it   50
  Merely an ass in 's foot-cloth, – [*To* CAMILLO.] how now
      brother –
  What travailing to bed to your kind wife?

CAMILLO. I assure you brother no. My voyage lies
  More northerly, in a far colder clime, –
  I do not well remember I protest   55
  When I last lay with her.

FLAMINEO. Strange you should lose your count.

CAMILLO. We never lay together but ere morning
  There grew a flaw between us.

FLAMINEO.   'T had been your part
  To have made up that flaw.

CAMILLO.   True, but she loathes   60
  I should be seen in 't.

FLAMINEO.   Why sir, what's the matter?

CAMILLO. The duke your master visits me – I thank him,
  And I perceive how like an earnest bowler
  He very passionately leans that way
  He should have his bowl run –

FLAMINEO.   I hope you do not think –   65

CAMILLO. That noblemen bowl booty? Faith his cheek
    Hath a most excellent bias, it would fain
    Jump with my mistress.

FLAMINEO.   Will you be an ass,
    Despite your Aristotle or a cuckold
    Contrary to your ephemerides   70
    Which shows you under what a smiling planet
    You were first swaddled?

CAMILLO.   Pew wew, sir tell not me
    Of planets nor of ephemerides –
    A man may be made cuckold in the day-time
    When the stars' eyes are out.

FLAMINEO.   Sir God boy you,   75
    I do commit you to your pitiful pillow
    Stuff'd with horn-shavings.

CAMILLO.   Brother.

FLAMINEO.   God refuse me,
    Might I advise you now your only course
    Were to lock up your wife.

CAMILLO.   'Twere very good.

FLAMINEO. Bar her the sight of revels.

CAMILLO.   Excellent.   80

FLAMINEO. Let her not go to church, but like a hound
    In leon at your heels.

CAMILLO.   'Twere for her honour –

FLAMINEO. And so you should be certain in one fortnight,
    Despite her chastity or innocence
    To be cuckolded, which yet is in suspense: 85
    This is my counsel and I ask no fee for 't.

CAMILLO. Come you know not where my night-cap wrings me.

FLAMINEO. Wear it a' th' old fashion, let your large ears come
    through, it will be more easy, – nay I will be bitter, – bar

your wife of her entertainment: women are more willingly   90
and more gloriously chaste, when they are least restrained
of their liberty. It seems you would be a fine capricious
mathematically jealous coxcomb, take the height of your
own horns with a Jacob's staff afore they are up. These
politic enclosures for paltry mutton makes more rebellion   95
in the flesh than all the provocative electuaries doctors have
uttered since last Jubilee.

CAMILLO. This doth not physic me.

FLAMINEO. It seems you are jealous, – I'll show you the
error of it by a familiar example, – I have seen a pair of   100
spectacles fashion'd with such perspective art, that lay down
but one twelvepence a' th' board 'twill appear as if there
were twenty, – now should you wear a pair of these spectacles, and see your wife tying her shoe, you would
imagine twenty hands were taking up of your wife's   105
clothes, and this would put you into a horrible cause-
less fury, –

CAMILLO. The fault there sir is not in the eye-sight –

FLAMINEO. True, but they that have the yellow jaundice,
think all objects they look on to be yellow. Jealousy is   110
worser, her fits present to a man, like so many bubbles
in a basin of water, twenty several crabbed faces, – many
times makes his own shadow his cuckold-maker.

Enter [VITTORIA] COROMBONA.

See she comes, – what reason have you to be jealous of
this creature? what an ignorant ass or flattering knave   115
might he be counted, that should write sonnets to her
eyes, or call her brow the snow of Ida, or ivory of
Corinth, or compare her hair to the blackbird's bill,
when 'tis liker the blackbird's feather. This is all: be
wise, I will make you friends and you shall go to bed to-   120
gether, – marry look you, it shall not be your seeking, do
you stand upon that by any means, – walk you aloof,
I would not have you seen in 't, – sister (my lord attends
you in the banqueting-house), your husband is wondrous discontented.   125

VITTORIA. I did nothing to displease him, I carved to him
    at supper-time –

FLAMINEO. (You need not have carved him in faith, they say
    he is a capon already, – I must now seemingly fall out with
    you.) Shall a gentleman so well descended as Camillo (a   130
    lousy slave that within this twenty years rode with the black
    guard in the duke's carriage 'mongst spits and dripping-
    pans) –

CAMILLO. Now he begins to tickle her.

FLAMINEO. An excellent scholar, (one that hath a head   135
    fill'd with calves' brains without any sage in them), come
    crouching in the hams to you for a night's lodging? –
    (that hath an itch in 's hams, which like the fire at the
    glass-house hath not gone out this seven years) – is he
    not a courtly gentleman? (when he wears white satin   140
    one would take him by his black muzzle to be no other
    creature than a maggot), – you are a goodly foil, I confess,
    well set out (but cover'd with a false stone – yon counterfeit
    diamond).

CAMILLO. He will make her know what is in me.   145

FLAMINEO [aside to VITTORIA]. Come, my lord attends you,
    thou shalt go to bed to my lord.

CAMILLO. Now he comes to 't.

FLAMINEO. With a relish as curious as a vintner going to taste new
    wine, – [To CAMILLO.] I am opening your case hard.   150

CAMILLO. A virtuous brother a' my credit.

FLAMINEO. He will give thee a ring with a philosopher's stone in it.

CAMILLO. Indeed I am studying alchemy.

FLAMINEO. Thou shalt lie in a bed stuff'd with turtles' feathers,
    swoon in perfumed linen like the fellow was smothered   155
    in roses, – so perfect shall be thy happiness, that as men
    at sea think land and trees and ships go that way they go,
    so both heaven and earth shall seem to go your voyage.

Shalt meet him, 'tis fix'd, with nails of diamonds to
inevitable necessity.   160

VITTORIA [*aside to* FLAMINEO]. How shall's rid him hence?

FLAMINEO [*aside to* VITTORIA]. I will put breese in 's tail,
set him gadding presently, – [*To* CAMILLO.] I have almost
wrought her to it, – I find her coming, but – might I advise
you now – for this night I would not lie with her, I would   165
cross her humour to make her more humble.

CAMILLO. Shall I, shall I?

FLAMINEO. It will show in you a supremacy of judgement.

CAMILLO. True, and a mind differing from the tumultuary
opinion, for *quæ negata grata*.   170

FLAMINEO. Right – you are the adamant shall draw her to
you, though you keep distance off: –

CAMILLO. A philosophical reason.

FLAMINEO. Walk by her a' the nobleman's fashion, and tell
her you will lie with her at the end of the progress –   175

CAMILLO. Vittoria, I cannot be induc'd, or as a man would
say incited . . .

VITTORIA. To do what sir?

CAMILLO. To lie with you tonight; your silkworm useth to
fast every third day, and the next following spins the better. 180
Tomorrow at night I am for you.

VITTORIA. You'll spin a fair thread, trust to 't.

FLAMINEO. But do you hear – I shall have you steal to her
chamber about midnight.

CAMILLO. Do you think so? why look you brother,   185
because you shall not think I'll gull you, take the key, lock
me into the chamber, and say you shall be sure of me.

FLAMINEO. In troth I will, I'll be your gaoler once, –
But have you ne'er a false door?

CAMILLO. A pox on 't, as I am a Christian – tell me   190 tomorrow how scurvily she takes my unkind parting –

FLAMINEO. I will.

CAMILLO. Didst thou not mark the jest of the silkworm?
goodnight – in faith I will use this trick often, –

FLAMINEO. Do, do, do.   195

Exit CAMILLO.

So now you are safe. Ha ha ha, thou entanglest thyself in
thine own work like a silkworm –

Enter BRACCIANO.

Come sister, darkness hides your blush, – women are like
curst dogs, civility keeps them tied all daytime, but they are
let loose at midnight, then they do most good or most mis-   200
chief, – my lord, my lord –

BRACCIANO. Give credit: I could wish time would stand still
And never end this interview, this hour,
But all delight doth itself soon'st devour.

*ZANCHE brings out a carpet, spreads it and lays on two fair
cushions. Enter* CORNELIA [*listening, behind*].

Let me into your bosom happy lady,   205
Pour out instead of eloquence my vows, –
Loose me not madam, for if you forego me
I am lost eternally.

VITTORIA.   Sir in the way of pity
I wish you heart-whole.

BRACCIANO.   You are a sweet physician.

VITTORIA. Sure sir a loathed cruelty in ladies   210
Is as to doctors many funerals:
It takes away their credit.

BRACCIANO.   Excellent creature.
We call the cruel fair, what name for you
That are so merciful?

ZANCHE.   See now they close.

FLAMINEO. Most happy union.   215

CORNELIA [*aside*]. My fears are fall'n upon me, O my heart!
    My son the pandar: now I find our house
    Sinking to ruin. Earthquakes leave behind,
    Where they have tyrannized, iron, or lead, or stone,
    But – woe to ruin – violent lust leaves none.   220

BRACCIANO. What value is this jewel?

VITTORIA.   'Tis the ornament
    Of a weak fortune.

BRACCIANO. In sooth I'll have it; nay I will but change
    My jewel for your jewel.

FLAMINEO.   Excellent,
    His jewel for her jewel, – well put in duke.   225

BRACCIANO. Nay let me see you wear it.

VITTORIA.   Here sir.

BRACCIANO. Nay lower, you shall wear my jewel lower.

FLAMINEO. That's better – she must wear his jewel lower.

VITTORIA. To pass away the time I'll tell your grace,
    A dream I had last night.

BRACCIANO.   Most wishedly.   230

VITTORIA. A foolish idle dream, –
    Methought I walk'd about the mid of night,
    Into a church-yard, where a goodly yew-tree
    Spread her large root in ground, – under that yew,
    As I sat sadly leaning on a grave,   235
    Chequered with cross-sticks, there came stealing in
    Your duchess and my husband, one of them
    A pick-axe bore, th' other a rusty spade,
    And in rough terms they gan to challenge me,
    About this yew.

BRACCIANO.   That tree.

VITTORIA.   This harmless yew.   240
    They told me my intent was to root up

That well-grown yew, and plant i' th' stead of it
A withered blackthorn, and for that they vow'd
To bury me alive: my husband straight
With pick-axe gan to dig, and your fell duchess   245
With shovel, like a Fury, voided out
The earth and scattered bones, – Lord how methought
I trembled, and yet for all this terror
I could not pray.

FLAMINEO. No the devil was in your dream.   250

VITTORIA. When to my rescue there arose methought
A whirlwind, which let fall a massy arm
From that strong plant,
And both were struck dead by that sacred yew
In that base shallow grave that was their due.   255

FLAMINEO. Excellent devil.
She hath taught him in a dream
To make away his duchess and her husband.

BRACCIANO. Sweetly shall I interpret this your dream, –
You are lodged within his arms who shall protect you,   260
From all the fevers of a jealous husband,
From the poor envy of our phlegmatic duchess, –
I'll seat you above law and above scandal,
Give to your thoughts the invention of delight
And the fruition, – nor shall government   265
Divide me from you longer than a care
To keep you great: you shall to me at once
Be dukedom, health, wife, children, friends and all.

CORNELIA [*coming forward*]. Woe to light hearts – they still forerun
    our fall.

FLAMINEO. What Fury rais'd thee up? away, away!

    Exit ZANCHE.   270

CORNELIA. What make you here my lord this dead of night?
    Never dropt mildew on a flower here,
    Till now.

FLAMINEO. I pray will you go to bed then,

Lest you be blasted?

CORNELIA.   O that this fair garden
    Had with all poisoned herbs of Thessaly   275
    At first been planted, made a nursery
    For witchcraft; rather than a burial plot,
    For both your honours.

VITTORIA.   Dearest mother hear me.

CORNELIA. O thou dost make thy brow bend to the earth,
    Sooner than nature, – see the curse of children!   280
    In life they keep us frequently in tears,
    And in the cold grave leave us in pale fears.

BRACCIANO. Come, come, I will not hear you.

VITTORIA.   Dear my lord.

CORNELIA. Where is thy duchess now adulterous duke?
    Thou little dream'd'st this night she is come to Rome.   285

FLAMINEO. How? come to Rome, –

VITTORIA.   The duchess, –

BRACCIANO.   She had been better, –

CORNELIA. The lives of princes should like dials move,
    Whose regular example is so strong,
    They make the times by them go right or wrong.

FLAMINEO. So, have you done?

CORNELIA.   Unfortunate Camillo.   290

VITTORIA. I do protest if any chaste denial,
    If anything but blood could have allayed
    His long suit to me, –

CORNELIA.   I will join with thee,
    To the most woeful end e'er mother kneel'd, –
    If thou dishonour thus thy husband's bed,   295
    Be thy life short as are the funeral tears
    In great men's, –

BRACCIANO.   Fie, fie, the woman's mad.

CORNELIA. Be thy act Judas-like – betray in kissing,
   May'st thou be envied during his short breath,
   And pitied like a wretch after his death.   300

VITTORIA. O me accurst.

   Exit VITTORIA.

FLAMINEO [*to Cornelia*]. Are you out of your wits? My lord,
   I'll fetch her back again.

BRACCIANO.   No I'll to bed.
   Send Doctor Julio to me presently, –
   Uncharitable woman thy rash tongue   305
   Hath rais'd a fearful and prodigious storm, –
   Be thou the cause of all ensuing harm.

   Exit BRACCIANO.

FLAMINEO. Now, you that stand so much upon your honour,
   Is this a fitting time a' night think you,
   To send a duke home without e'er a man?   310
   I would fain know where lies the mass of wealth
   Which you have hoarded for my maintenance,
   That I may bear my beard out of the level
   Of my lord's stirrup.

CORNELIA.   What? because we are poor,
   Shall we be vicious?

FLAMINEO.   Pray what means have you   315
   To keep me from the galleys, or the gallows?
   My father prov'd himself a gentleman,
   Sold all's land, and like a fortunate fellow,
   Died ere the money was spent. You brought me up
   At Padua I confess, where I protest   320
   For want of means, – the university judge me, –
   I have been fain to heel my tutor's stockings
   At least seven years: conspiring with a beard
   Made me a graduate, – then to this duke's service:
   I visited the court, whence I return'd,   325
   More courteous, more lecherous by far,
   But not a suit the richer, – and shall I,

Having a path so open and so free
To my preferment, still retain your milk
In my pale forehead? no this face of mine   330
I'll arm and fortify with lusty wine
'Gainst shame and blushing.

CORNELIA. O that I ne'er had borne thee, –

FLAMINEO.   So would I.
I would the common'st courtezan in Rome
Had been my mother rather than thyself.   335
Nature is very pitiful to whores
To give them but few children, yet those children
Plurality of fathers, – they are sure
They shall not want. Go, go,
Complain unto my great lord cardinal,   340
Yet may be he will justify the act.
Lycurgus wond'red much men would provide
Good stallions for their mares, and yet would suffer
Their fair wives to be barren.

CORNELIA. Misery of miseries.   345

Exit CORNELIA.

FLAMINEO. The duchess come to court, I like not that, –
We are engag'd to mischief and must on:
As rivers to find out the ocean
Flow with crook bendings beneath forced banks,
Or as we see, to aspire some mountain's top,   350
The way ascends not straight, but imitates
The subtle foldings of a winter's snake,
So who knows policy and her true aspect,
Shall find her ways winding and indirect.

Exit.

Act Two, Scene One

Enter FRANCISCO DE MEDICI, *Cardinal* MONTICELSO,
MARCELLO, ISABELLA, *young* GIOVANNI, *with*
ATTENDANTS.

FRANCISCO. Have you not seen your husband since you arrived?

ISABELLA. Not yet sir.

FRANCISCO.   Surely he is wondrous kind, –
   If I had such a dove-house as Camillo's
   I would set fire on 't, were 't but to destroy
   The pole-cats that haunt to 't, – my sweet cousin.   5

GIOVANNI. Lord uncle you did promise me a horse
   And armour.

FRANCISCO.   That I did my pretty cousin, –
   Marcello see it fitted.

MARCELLO. My lord – the duke is here.

FRANCISCO.   Sister away –
   You must not yet be seen.

ISABELLA.   I do beseech you   10
   Entreat him mildly, let not your rough tongue
   Set us at louder variance, – all my wrongs
   Are freely pardoned, and I do not doubt
   As men to try the precious unicorn's horn
   Make of the powder a preservative circle   15
   And in it put a spider, so these arms
   Shall charm his poison, force it to obeying
   And keep him chaste from an infected straying.

FRANCISCO. I wish it may. Be gone.

   Exit [ISABELLA]. *Enter* BRACCIANO, *and* FLAMINEO.

                                        Void the chamber, –

[*Exeunt* FLAMINEO, MARCELLO, GIOVANNI, *and*
ATTENDANTS.]

You are welcome, will you sit? I pray my lord   20
Be you my orator, my heart's too full, –
I'll second you anon.

MONTICELSO.   Ere I begin
Let me entreat your grace forego all passion
Which may be raised by my free discourse.

BRACCIANO. As silent as i' th' church – you may proceed.   25

MONTICELSO. It is a wonder to your noble friends,
That you that have as 'twere ent'red the world
With a free sceptre in your able hand,
And have to th' use of nature well applied
High gifts of learning, should in your prime age   30
Neglect your awful throne, for the soft down
Of an insatiate bed. O my lord,
The drunkard after all his lavish cups,
Is dry, and then is sober, so at length,
When you awake from this lascivious dream,   35
Repentance then will follow; like the sting
Plac'd in the adder's tail: wretched are princes
When fortune blasteth but a petty flower
Of their unwieldy crowns; or ravisheth
But one pearl from their sceptre: but alas!   40
When they to wilful shipwreck loose good fame
All princely titles perish with their name.

BRACCIANO. You have said my lord, –

MONTICELSO.   Enough to give you taste
How far I am from flattering your greatness?

BRACCIANO. Now you that are his second, what say you?   45
Do not like young hawks fetch a course about –
Your game flies fair and for you, –

FRANCISCO.   Do not fear it:
I'll answer you in your own hawking phrase, –

Some eagles that should gaze upon the sun
Seldom soar high, but take their lustful ease,   50
Since they from dunghill birds their prey can seize, –
You know Vittoria, –

BRACCIANO.   Yes.

FRANCISCO.   You shift your shirt there
When you retire from tennis.

BRACCIANO.   Happily.

FRANCISCO. Her husband is lord of a poor fortune
Yet she wears cloth of tissue, –

BRACCIANO.   What of this?   55
Will you urge that my good lord cardinal
As part of her confession at next shrift,
And know from whence it sails?

FRANCISCO.   She is your strumpet, –

BRACCIANO. Uncivil sir there's hemlock in thy breath
And that black slander, – were she a whore of mine   60
All thy loud cannons, and thy borrowed Switzers,
Thy galleys, nor thy sworn confederates,
Durst not supplant her.

FRANCISCO.   Let's not talk on thunder, –
Thou hast a wife, our sister, – would I had given
Both her white hands to death, bound and lock'd fast   65
In her last winding-sheet, when I gave thee
But one.

BRACCIANO. Thou hadst given a soul to God then.

FRANCISCO.   True.
Thy ghostly father with all 's absolution,
Shall ne'er do so by thee.

BRACCIANO.   Spit thy poison, –

FRANCISCO. I shall not need, lust carries her sharp whip   70
At her own girdle, – look to 't for our anger
Is making thunder-bolts.

BRACCIANO.   Thunder? in faith,
    They are but crackers.

FRANCISCO.   We'll end this with the cannon.

BRACCIANO. Thou'lt get nought by it but iron in thy wounds,
    And gunpowder in thy nostrils.

FRANCISCO.   Better that   75
    Than change perfumes for plasters, –

BRACCIANO.   Pity on thee,
    'Twere good you'd show your slaves or men condemn'd
    Your new-plough'd forehead – Defiance! – and I'll meet thee,
    Even in a thicket of thy ablest men.

MONTICELSO. My lords, you shall not word it any further   80
    Without a milder limit.

FRANCISCO.   Willingly.

BRACCIANO. Have you proclaimed a triumph that you bait
    A lion thus?

MONTICELSO. My lord.

BRACCIANO.   I am tame, I am tame sir.

FRANCISCO. We send unto the duke for conference
    'Bout levies 'gainst the pirates, my lord duke   85
    Is not at home, – we come ourself in person,
    Still my lord duke is busied, – but we fear
    When Tiber to each prowling passenger
    Discovers flocks of wild ducks, then my lord –
    'Bout moulting time I mean, – we shall be certain   90
    To find you sure enough and speak with you.

BRACCIANO.   Ha?

FRANCISCO. A mere tale of a tub, my words are idle, –
    But to express the sonnet by natural reason,

    Enter GIOVANNI.

    When stags grow melancholic you'll find the season –

MONTICELSO. No more my lord, here comes a champion   95

Shall end the difference between you both,
Your son the prince Giovanni, – see my lords
What hopes you store in him, this is a casket
For both your crowns, and should be held like dear:
Now is he apt for knowledge, therefore know   100
It is a more direct and even way
To train to virtue those of princely blood,
By examples than by precepts: if by examples
Whom should he rather strive to imitate
Than his own father? be his pattern then,   105
Leave him a stock of virtue that may last,
Should fortune rend his sails, and split his mast.

BRACCIANO. Your hand boy – growing to a soldier?

GIOVANNI. Give me a pike.

FRANCISCO. What practising your pike so young, fair coz?   110

GIOVANNI. Suppose me one of Homer's frogs, my lord,
Tossing my bulrush thus, – pray sir tell me
Might not a child of good discretion
Be leader to an army?

FRANCISCO.   Yes cousin a young prince
Of good discretion might.

GIOVANNI.   Say you so, –   115
Indeed I have heard 'tis fit a general
Should not endanger his own person oft,
So that he make a noise, when he's a' horseback
Like a Dansk drummer, – O 'tis excellent!
He need not fight, methinks his horse as well   120
Might lead an army for him; if I live
I'll charge the French foe, in the very front
Of all my troops, the foremost man.

FRANCISCO.   What, what, –

GIOVANNI. And will not bid my soldiers up and follow
But bid them follow me.

BRACCIANO.   Forward lapwing   125
He flies with the shell on's head.

FRANCISCO.   Pretty cousin, –

GIOVANNI. The first year uncle that I go to war,
    All prisoners that I take I will set free
    Without their ransom.

FRANCISCO.   Ha, without their ransom, –
    How then will you reward your soldiers   130
    That took those prisoners for you?

GIOVANNI.   Thus my lord
    I'll marry them to all the wealthy widows
    That fall that year.

FRANCISCO.   Why then the next year following
    You'll have no men to go with you to war.

GIOVANNI. Why then I'll press the women to the war,   135
    And then the men will follow.

MONTICELSO.   Witty prince.

FRANCISCO. See a good habit makes a child a man,
    Whereas a bad one makes a man a beast:
    Come you and I are friends.

BRACCIANO.   Most wishedly,
    Like bones which broke in sunder and well set   140
    Knit the more strongly.

FRANCISCO [to ATTENDANT off-stage]. Call Camillo hither –
    You have received the rumour, how Count Lodowick
    Is turn'd a pirate.

BRACCIANO.   Yes.

FRANCISCO.   We are now preparing
    Some ships to fetch him in:

    [Enter ISABELLA.]

                                behold your duchess, –
    We now will leave you and expect from you   145
    Nothing but kind entreaty.

BRACCIANO.   You have charm'd me.

Exeunt FRANCISCO, MONTICELSO, GIOVANNI.

You are in health we see.

ISABELLA.   And above health
To see my lord well, –

BRACCIANO.   So – I wonder much
What amorous whirlwind hurried you to Rome –

ISABELLA. Devotion my lord.

BRACCIANO.   Devotion?   150
Is your soul charg'd with any grievous sin?

ISABELLA. 'Tis burdened with too many, and I think
The oft'ner that we cast our reckonings up,
Our sleeps will be the sounder.

BRACCIANO.   Take your chamber.

ISABELLA. Nay my dear lord I will not have you angry, –   155
Doth not my absence from you two months
Merit one kiss?

BRACCIANO.   I do not use to kiss, –
If that will dispossess your jealousy,
I'll swear it to you.

ISABELLA.   O my loved lord,
I do not come to chide; my jealousy?   160
I am to learn what that Italian means, –
You are as welcome to these longing arms
As I to you a virgin.

BRACCIANO.   O your breath!
Out upon sweet meats, and continued physic!
The plague is in them.

ISABELLA.   You have oft for these two lips   165
Neglected cassia or the natural sweets
Of the spring violet, – they are not yet much withered, –
My lord I should be merry, – these your frowns
Show in a helmet lovely, but on me,
In such a peaceful interview methinks   170
They are too too roughly knit.

BRACCIANO.   O dissemblance!
  Do you bandy factions 'gainst me? have you learnt
  The trick of impudent baseness to complain
  Unto your kindred?

ISABELLA.   Never my dear lord.

BRACCIANO. Must I be haunted out, or was 't your trick   175
  To meet some amorous gallant here in Rome
  That must supply our discontinuance?

ISABELLA. I pray sir burst my heart, and in my death
  Turn to your ancient pity, though not love.

BRACCIANO. Because your brother is the corpulent duke,   180
  That is the great duke, – 'Sdeath I shall not shortly
  Racket away five hundred crowns at tennis,
  But it shall rest upon record: I scorn him
  Like a shav'd Polack, – all his reverend wit
  Lies in his wardrobe, he's a discreet fellow   185
  When he's made up in his robes of state, –
  Your brother the great duke, because h' as galleys,
  And now and then ransacks a Turkish fly-boat,
  (Now all the hellish Furies take his soul,)
  First made this match, – accursed be the priest   190
  That sang the wedding mass, and even my issue.

ISABELLA. O too too far you have curs'd.

BRACCIANO.   Your hand I'll kiss, –
  This is the latest ceremony of my love,
  Henceforth I'll never lie with thee, by this,
  This wedding-ring: I'll ne'er more lie with thee.   195
  And this divorce shall be as truly kept,
  As if the judge had doom'd it: fare you well,
  Our sleeps are sever'd.

ISABELLA.   Forbid it the sweet union
  Of all things blessed; why the saints in heaven
  Will knit their brows at that.

BRACCIANO.   Let not thy love   200
  Make thee an unbeliever, – this my vow

Shall never, on my soul, be satisfied
With my repentance: let thy brother rage
Beyond a horrid tempest or sea-fight,
My vow is fixed.

ISABELLA.   O my winding-sheet,   205
Now shall I need thee shortly! dear my lord,
Let me hear once more, what I would not hear, –
Never?

BRACCIANO. Never.

ISABELLA. O my unkind lord may your sins find mercy,   210
As I upon a woeful widowed bed
Shall pray for you, if not to turn your eyes
Upon your wretched wife, and hopeful son,
Yet that in time you'll fix them upon heaven.

BRACCIANO. No more, – go, go, complain to the great duke. 215

ISABELLA. No my dear lord, you shall have present witness
How I'll work peace between you, – I will make
Myself the author of your cursed vow –
I have some cause to do it, you have none, –
Conceal it I beseech you, for the weal   220
Of both your dukedoms, that you wrought the means
Of such a separation, let the fault
Remain with my supposed jealousy, –
And think with what a piteous and rent heart,
I shall perform this sad ensuing part.   225

Enter FRANCISCO, FLAMINEO, MONTICELSO,
MARCELLO.

BRACCIANO. Well, take your course – my honourable brother!

FRANCISCO. Sister, – this is not well my lord, – why sister! –
She merits not this welcome.

BRACCIANO.   Welcome say?
She hath given a sharp welcome.

FRANCISCO.   Are you foolish?
Come dry your tears, – is this a modest course,   230
To better what is nought, to rail and weep?

Grow to a reconcilement, or by heaven,
I'll ne'er more deal between you.

ISABELLA.   Sir you shall not,
   No though Vittoria upon that condition
   Would become honest.

FRANCISCO.   Was your husband loud,   235
   Since we departed?

ISABELLA.   By my life sir no, –
   I swear by that I do not care to lose.
   Are all these ruins of my former beauty
   Laid out for a whore's triumph?

FRANCISCO.   Do you hear? –
   Look upon other women, with what patience   240
   They suffer these slight wrongs, with what justice
   They study to requite them, – take that course.

ISABELLA. O that I were a man, or that I had power
   To execute my apprehended wishes,
   I would whip some with scorpions.

FRANCISCO.   What? turn'd Fury?   245

ISABELLA. To dig the strumpet's eyes out, let her lie
   Some twenty months a-dying, to cut off
   Her nose and lips, pull out her rotten teeth,
   Preserve her flesh like mummia, for trophies
   Of my just anger: hell to my affliction   250
   Is mere snow-water: by your favour sir, –
   Brother draw near, and my lord cardinal, –
   Sir let me borrow of you but one kiss,
   Henceforth I'll never lie with you, by this,
   This wedding-ring.

FRANCISCO.   How? ne'er more lie with him? –   255

ISABELLA. And this divorce shall be as truly kept,
   As if in thronged court, a thousand ears
   Had heard it, and a thousand lawyers' hands
   Seal'd to the separation.

BRACCIANO. Ne'er lie with me?

ISABELLA.   Let not my former dotage   260
  Make thee an unbeliever, – this my vow
  Shall never, on my soul, be satisfied
  With my repentance, – *manet alta mente repostum.*

FRANCISCO. Now by my birth you are a foolish, mad,
  And jealous woman.

BRACCIANO.   You see 'tis not my seeking.   265

FRANCISCO. Was this your circle of pure unicorn's horn
  You said should charm your lord? now horns upon thee,
  For jealousy deserves them, – keep your vow,
  And take your chamber.

ISABELLA. No sir I'll presently to Padua,   270
  I will not stay a minute.

MONTICELSO.   O good madam.

BRACCIANO. 'Twere best to let her have her humour,
  Some half day's journey will bring down her stomach,
  And then she'll turn in post.

FRANCISCO.   To see her come
  To my lord cardinal for a dispensation   275
  Of her rash vow will beget excellent laughter.

ISABELLA. Unkindness do thy office, poor heart break, –
  Those are the killing griefs which dare not speak.

  Exit. Enter CAMILLO.

MARCELLO. Camillo's come my lord.

FRANCISCO. Where's the commission?   280

MARCELLO. 'Tis here.

FRANCISCO. Give me the signet.

FLAMINEO [*to* BRACCIANO]. My lord, do you mark their
  whispering? I will compound a medicine out of their two
  heads, stronger than garlic, deadlier than stibium, – the   285
  cantharides which are scarce seen to stick upon the flesh
  when they work to the heart, shall not do it with more
  silence or invisible cunning.

Enter Doctor [JULIO].

BRACCIANO. About the murder.

FLAMINEO. They are sending him to Naples, but I'll send   290
    him to Candy, – here's another property too.

BRACCIANO. O the doctor, –

FLAMINEO. A poor quack-salving knave, my lord, one that
    should have been lash'd for 's lechery, but that he confess'd
    a judgement, had an execution laid upon him, and so put   295
    the whip to a *non plus*.

JULIO. And was cozen'd, my lord, by an arranter knave than
    myself, and made pay all the colourable execution.

FLAMINEO. He will shoot pills into a man's guts, shall make
    them have more ventages than a cornet or a lamprey, –   300
    he will poison a kiss, and was once minded, for his master-
    piece, because Ireland breeds no poison, to have prepared a
    deadly vapour in a Spaniard's fart that should have poison'd
    all Dublin.

BRACCIANO. O Saint Anthony's fire!   305

JULIO. Your secretary is merry my lord.

FLAMINEO. O thou cursed antipathy to nature, – look his
    eye's bloodshed like a needle a chirurgeon stitcheth a wound
    with, – let me embrace thee toad, and love thee O thou
    abhominable loathsome gargarism, that will fetch up   310
    lungs, lights, heart, and liver by scruples.

BRACCIANO. No more, – I must employ thee honest doctor,
    You must to Padua and by the way,
    Use some of your skill for us.

JULIO.   Sir I shall.

BRACCIANO. But for Camillo?   315

FLAMINEO. He dies this night by such a politic strain,
    Men shall suppose him by 's own engine slain.
    But for your duchess' death?

JULIO.   I'll make her sure –

BRACCIANO. Small mischiefs are by greater made secure.

FLAMINEO. Remember this you slave, – when knaves come   320
  to preferment they rise as gallowses are raised i' th' Low
  Countries, one upon another's shoulders.

  Exeunt [BRACCIANO, FLAMINEO, *and Doctor* JULIO].

MONTICELSO. Here is an emblem nephew – pray peruse it.
  'Twas thrown in at your window, –

CAMILLO.   At my window?
  Here is a stag my lord hath shed his horns,   325
  And for the loss of them the poor beast weeps –
  The word '*Inopem me copia fecit*'.

MONTICELSO. That is,
  Plenty of horns hath made him poor of horns.

CAMILLO. What should this mean?

MONTICELSO.   I'll tell you, – 'tis given out
  You are a cuckold.

CAMILLO.   Is it given out so?   331
  I had rather such report as that, my lord,
  Should keep within doors.

FRANCISCO.   Have you any children?

CAMILLO. None my lord.

FRANCISCO.   You are the happier –
  I'll tell you a tale.

CAMILLO.   Pray my lord.

FRANCISCO.   An old tale.   335
  Upon a time Phoebus the god of light
  (Or him we call the sun) would need be married.
  The gods gave their consent, and Mercury
  Was sent to voice it to the general world.
  But what a piteous cry there straight arose   340
  Amongst smiths, and felt-makers, brewers and cooks,
  Reapers and butter-women, amongst fishmongers
  And thousand other trades, which are annoyed

By his excessive heat; 'twas lamentable.
They came to Jupiter all in a sweat   345
And do forbid the bans; a great fat cook
Was made their speaker, who entreats of Jove
That Phoebus might be gelded, for if now
When there was but one sun, so many men
Were like to perish by his violent heat,   350
What should they do if he were married
And should beget more, and those children
Make fireworks like their father? – so say I,
Only I will apply it to your wife, –
Her issue (should not providence prevent it)   355
Would make both nature, time, and man repent it.

MONTICELSO. Look you cousin,
Go change the air for shame, see if your absence
Will blast your cornucopia, – Marcello
Is chosen with you joint commissioner   360
For the relieving our Italian coast
From pirates.

MARCELLO.   I am much honour'd in 't.

CAMILLO.   But sir
Ere I return the stag's horns may be sprouted,
Greater than these are shed.

MONTICELSO.   Do not fear it,
I'll be your ranger.

CAMILLO.   You must watch i' th' nights,   365
Then's the most danger.

FRANCISCO.   Farewell good Marcello.
All the best fortunes of a soldier's wish
Bring you a' ship-board.

CAMILLO. Were I not best now I am turn'd soldier,
Ere that I leave my wife, sell all she hath,   370
And then take leave of her?

MONTICELSO.   I expect good from you,
Your parting is so merry.

CAMILLO. Merry my lord, a' th' captain's humour right –
    I am resolved to be drunk this night.

Exit [CAMILLO *with* MARCELLO].

FRANCISCO. So, – 'twas well fitted, now shall we discern   375
    How his wish'd absence will give violent way
    To Duke Bracciano's lust, –

MONTICELSO.   Why that was it;
    To what scorn'd purpose else should we make choice
    Of him for a sea-captain? and besides,
    Count Lodowick which was rumour'd for a pirate,   380
    Is now in Padua.

FRANCISCO.   Is 't true?

MONTICELSO.   Most certain.
    I have letters from him, which are suppliant
    To work his quick repeal from banishment, –
    He means to address himself for pension
    Unto our sister duchess.

FRANCISCO.   O 'twas well.   385
    We shall not want his absence past six days, –
    I fain would have the Duke Bracciano run
    Into notorious scandal, for there's nought
    In such curst dotage, to repair his name,
    Only the deep sense of some deathless shame.   390

MONTICELSO. It may be objected I am dishonourable,
    To play thus with my kinsman, but I answer,
    For my revenge I'd stake a brother's life,
    That being wrong'd durst not avenge himself.   394

FRANCISCO. Come to observe this strumpet.

MONTICELSO.   Curse of greatness, –
    Sure he'll not leave her.

FRANCISCO.   There's small pity in 't –
    Like mistletoe on sere elms spent by weather,
    Let him cleave to her and both rot together.

Exeunt.

Act Two, Scene Two

Enter BRACCIANO *with one in the habit of a* CONJURER.

BRACCIANO. Now sir I claim your promise, – 'tis dead midnight,
    The time prefix'd to show me by your art
    How the intended murder of Camillo,
    And our loathed duchess grow to action.

CONJURER. You have won me by your bounty to a deed   5
    I do not often practise, – some there are,
    Which by sophistic tricks, aspire that name
    Which I would gladly lose, of nigromancer;
    As some that use to juggle upon cards,
    Seeming to conjure, when indeed they cheat: 10
    Others that raise up their confederate spirits
    'Bout windmills, and endanger their own necks,
    For making of a squib, and some there are
    Will keep a curtal to show juggling tricks
    And give out 'tis a spirit: besides these   15
    Such a whole ream of almanac-makers, figure-flingers, –
    Fellows indeed that only live by stealth,
    Since they do merely lie about stol'n goods, –
    They'd make men think the devil were fast and loose,
    With speaking fustian Latin: pray sit down,   20
    Put on this night-cap sir, 'tis charm'd, – and now
    I'll show you by my strong-commanding art
    The circumstance that breaks your duchess' heart.

A dumb show.

Enter suspiciously, JULIO *and another, they draw a curtain where*
BRACCIANO'*s picture is, they put on spectacles of glass, which*
cover their eyes and noses, and then burn perfumes afore the picture,
and wash the lips of the picture, that done, quenching the fire, and
putting off their spectacles they depart laughing.

Enter ISABELLA *in her nightgown as to bed-ward, with lights after*

*her, Count LODOVICO, GIOVANNI, and others waiting on
her, she kneels down as to prayers, then draws the curtain of the picture,
does three reverences to it, and kisses it thrice, she faints and will not
suffer them to come near it, dies; sorrow express'd in GIOVANNI
and in Count LODOVICO; she's convey'd out solemnly.*

BRACCIANO. Excellent, then she's dead, –

CONJURER.   She's poisoned,
By the fum'd picture, – 'twas her custom nightly,   25
Before she went to bed, to go and visit
Your picture, and to feed her eyes and lips
On the dead shadow, – Doctor Julio
Observing this, infects it with an oil
And other poison'd stuff, which presently   30
Did suffocate her spirits.

BRACCIANO.   Methought I saw
Count Lodowick there.

CONJURER.   He was, and by my art
I find he did most passionately dote
Upon your duchess, – now turn another way,
And view Camillo's far more politic fate, –   35
Strike louder music from this charmed ground,
To field, as fits the act, a tragic sound.

The second dumb show.

*Enter FLAMINEO, MARCELLO, CAMILLO, with four more as
Captains, they drink healths and dance, a vaulting-horse is brought into the
room; MARCELLO and two more whisper'd out of the room while
FLAMINEO and CAMILLO strip themselves into their shirts, as to
vault; compliment who shall begin, as CAMILLO is about to vault,
FLAMINEO pitcheth him upon his neck, and with the help of the rest,
writhes his neck about, seems to see if it be broke, and lays him folded double
as 'twere under the horse, makes shows to call for help; MARCELLO
comes in, laments, sends for the Cardinal [MONTICELSO] and Duke
[FRANCISCO], who comes forth with armed men; wonder at the act;
[FRANCISCO] commands the body to be carried home, apprehends
FLAMINEO, MARCELLO, and the rest, and [all] go as 'twere to
apprehend VITTORIA.*

BRACCIANO. 'Twas quaintly done, but yet each circumstance
   I taste not fully.

CONJURER.   O 'twas most apparent,
   You saw them enter charged with their deep healths   40
   To their boon voyage, and to second that,
   Flamineo calls to have a vaulting-horse
   Maintain their sport. The virtuous Marcello
   Is innocently plotted forth the room,
   Whilst your eye saw the rest, and can inform you   45
   The engine of all.

BRACCIANO. It seems Marcello, and Flamineo
   Are both committed.

CONJURER.   Yes, you saw them guarded,
   And now they are come with purpose to apprehend
   Your mistress, fair Vittoria; we are now   50
   Beneath her roof: 'twere fit we instantly
   Make out by some back postern: –

BRACCIANO.   Noble friend,
   You bind me ever to you, – this shall stand
   As the firm seal annexed to my hand.
   It shall enforce a payment.

CONJURER.   Sir I thank you.   55

Exit BRACCIANO.

Both flowers and weeds spring when the sun is warm,
And great men do great good, or else great harm.

Exit CONJURER.

Act Three, Scene One

Enter FRANCISCO, *and* MONTICELSO, *their* CHANCELLOR
and REGISTER.

FRANCISCO. You have dealt discreetly to obtain the presence
    Of all the grave lieger ambassadors
    To hear Vittoria's trial.

MONTICELSO.   'Twas not ill,
    For sir you know we have nought but circumstances
    To charge her with, about her husband's death, –   5
    Their approbation therefore to the proofs
    Of her black lust, shall make her infamous
    To all our neighbouring kingdoms, – I wonder
    If Bracciano will be here.

FRANCISCO.   O fie,
    'Twere impudence too palpable.   10

    [*Exeunt.*] *Enter* FLAMINEO *and* MARCELLO *guarded,*
    and a LAWYER.

LAWYER. What are you in by the week? so – I will try now
    whether thy wit be close prisoner, – methinks none should
    sit upon thy sister but old whore-masters, –

FLAMINEO. Or cuckolds, for your cuckold is your most
    terrible tickler of lechery: whore-masters would serve, for   15
    none are judges at tilting, but those that have been old tilters.

LAWYER. My lord duke and she have been very private.

FLAMINEO. You are a dull ass, 'tis threat'ned they have been very
    public.

LAWYER. If it can be proved they have but kiss'd one another.   20

FLAMINEO. What then?

LAWYER. My lord cardinal will ferret them, –

FLAMINEO. A cardinal I hope will not catch conies.

LAWYER. For to sow kisses (mark what I say) to sow kisses, is
    to reap lechery, and I am sure a woman that will endure   25
    kissing is half won.

FLAMINEO. True, her upper part by that rule, – if you will
    win her nether part too, you know what follows.

LAWYER. Hark the ambassadors are lighted, –

FLAMINEO [aside]. I do put on this feigned garb of mirth   30
    To gull suspicion.

MARCELLO. O my unfortunate sister!
    I would my dagger's point had cleft her heart
    When she first saw Bracciano: you 'tis said,
    Were made his engine, and his stalking horse   35
    To undo my sister.

FLAMINEO.   I made a kind of path
    To her and mine own preferment.

MARCELLO.   Your ruin.

FLAMINEO. Hum! thou art a soldier,
    Followest the great duke, feedest his victories,
    As witches do their serviceable spirits,   40
    Even with thy prodigal blood, – what hast got?
    But like the wealth of captains, a poor handful,
    Which in thy palm thou bear'st, as men hold water –
    Seeking to gripe it fast, the frail reward
    Steals through thy fingers.   44

MARCELLO.   Sir, –

FLAMINEO.   Thou hast scarce maintenance
    To keep thee in fresh chamois.

MARCELLO.   Brother!

FLAMINEO.   Hear me, –
    And thus when we have even poured ourselves
    Into great fights, for their ambition

Or idle spleen, how shall we find reward?
But as we seldom find the mistletoe   50
Sacred to physic on the builder oak
Without a mandrake by it, so in our quest of gain.
Alas the poorest of their forc'd dislikes
At a limb proffers, but at heart it strikes:
This is lamented doctrine.

MARCELLO. Come, come.   55

FLAMINEO.   When age shall turn thee
White as a blooming hawthorn, –

MARCELLO.   I'll interrupt you.
For love of virtue bear an honest heart,
And stride over every politic respect,
Which where they most advance they most infect.   60
Were I your father, as I am your brother,
I should not be ambitious to leave you
A better patrimony.

   Enter Savoy [AMBASSADOR].

FLAMINEO.   I'll think on 't, –
The lord ambassadors.

   Here there is a passage of the lieger AMBASSADORS *over the stage
   severally. Enter* FRENCH AMBASSADOR.

LAWYER. O my sprightly Frenchman, do you know him? he's   65
   an admirable tilter.

FLAMINEO. I saw him at last tilting, he showed like a pewter
   candlestick fashioned like a man in armour, holding a tilting
   staff in his hand, little bigger than a candle of twelve i' th'
   pound.   70

LAWYER. O but he's an excellent horseman.

FLAMINEO. A lame one in his lofty tricks, – he sleeps a' horseback
   like a poulter, –

   Enter ENGLISH *and* SPANISH [AMBASSADORS].

LAWYER. Lo you my Spaniard.

FLAMINEO. He carries his face in 's ruff, as I have seen a   75
    serving-man carry glasses in a cypress hat-band, monstrous
    steady for fear of breaking, – he looks like the claw of a
    blackbird, first salted and then broiled in a candle.

Exeunt.

Act Three, Scene Two

THE ARRAIGNMENT OF VITTORIA.

Enter FRANCISCO, MONTICELSO, *the six lieger*
AMBASSADORS, BRACCIANO, VITTORIA, [ZANCHE,
FLAMINEO, MARCELLO], LAWYER, *and a* GUARD.

MONTICELSO. Forbear my lord, here is no place assign'd you,
    This business by his holiness is left
    To our examination.

BRACCIANO.   May it thrive with you.

Lays a rich gown under him.

FRANCISCO. A chair there for his lordship.

BRACCIANO. Forbear your kindness, an unbidden guest   5
    Should travail as Dutch women go to church:
    Bear their stools with them.

MONTICELSO.   At your pleasure sir.
   Stand to the table gentlewoman: now signior
    Fall to your plea.

LAWYER. *Domine judex converte oculos in hanc pestem mulierum*   10
    corruptissimam.

VITTORIA. What's he?

FRANCISCO.   A lawyer, that pleads against you.

VITTORIA. Pray my lord, let him speak his usual tongue –
    I'll make no answer else.

FRANCISCO. Why you understand Latin.

VITTORIA. I do sir, but amongst this auditory   15
    Which come to hear my cause, the half or more
    May be ignorant in 't.

MONTICELSO.   Go on sir: −

VITTORIA.   By your favour,
    I will not have my accusation clouded
    In a strange tongue: all this assembly
    Shall hear what you can charge me with.

FRANCISCO.   Signior,   20
    You need not stand on 't much; pray change your language.

MONTICELSO. O for God sake: gentlewoman, your credit
    Shall be more famous by it.

LAWYER.   Well then have at you.

VITTORIA. I am at the mark sir, I'll give aim to you,
    And tell you how near you shoot.   25

LAWYER. Most literated judges, please your lordships,
    So to connive your judgements to the view
    Of this debauch'd and diversivolent woman
    Who such a black concatenation
    Of mischief hath effected, that to extirp   30
    The memory of 't, must be the consummation
    Of her and her projections −

VITTORIA.   What's all this −

LAWYER. Hold your peace.
    Exorbitant sins must have exulceration.

VITTORIA. Surely my lords this lawyer here hath swallowed   35
    Some pothecary's bills, or proclamations.
    And now the hard and undigestible words
    Come up like stones we use give hawks for physic.
    Why this is Welsh to Latin.

LAWYER.   My lords, the woman
    Knows not her tropes nor figures, nor is perfect   40
    In the academic derivation
    Of grammatical elocution.

FRANCISCO.   Sir your pains
    Shall be well spared, and your deep eloquence
    Be worthily applauded amongst those
    Which understand you.

LAWYER.   My good lord!

FRANCISCO.   Sir,   45
    Put up your papers in your fustian bag, –

FRANCISCO *speaks this as in scorn.*

    Cry mercy sir, 'tis buckram, – and accept
    My notion of your learn'd verbosity.

LAWYER. I most graduatically thank your lordship.
    I shall have use for them elsewhere. [*Exit.*]   50

MONTICELSO. I shall be plainer with you, and paint out
    Your follies in more natural red and white
    Than that upon your cheek.

VITTORIA.   O you mistake.
    You raise a blood as noble in this cheek
    As ever was your mother's.   55

MONTICELSO. I must spare you till proof cry whore to that;
    Observe this creature here my honoured lords,
    A woman of a most prodigious spirit
    In her effected.

VITTORIA.   Honourable my lord,
    It doth not suit a reverend cardinal   60
    To play the lawyer thus.

MONTICELSO. O your trade instructs your language!
    You see my lords what goodly fruit she seems,
    Yet like those apples travellers report
    To grow where Sodom and Gomorrah stood,   65
    I will but touch her and you straight shall see
    She'll fall to soot and ashes.

VITTORIA.   Your envenom'd
    Pothecary should do't.

MONTICELSO.   I am resolved

Were there a second paradise to lose
This devil would betray it.

VITTORIA.   O poor charity!   70
Thou art seldom found in scarlet.

MONTICELSO. Who knows not how, when several night by night
Her gates were chok'd with coaches, and her rooms
Outbrav'd the stars with several kind of lights,
When she did counterfeit a prince's court   75
In music, banquets and most riotous surfeits?
This whore, forsooth, was holy.

VITTORIA.   Ha? whore – what's that?

MONTICELSO. Shall I expound whore to you? sure I shall;
I'll give their perfect character. They are first,
Sweet-meats which rot the eater: in man's nostril   80
Poison'd perfumes. They are coz'ning alchemy,
Shipwrecks in calmest weather. What are whores?
Cold Russian winters, that appear so barren,
As if that nature had forgot the spring.
They are the true material fire of hell,   85
Worse than those tributes i' th' Low Countries paid,
Exactions upon meat, drink, garments, sleep;
Ay even on man's perdition, his sin.
They are those brittle evidences of law
Which forfeit all a wretched man's estate   90
For leaving out one syllable. What are whores?
They are those flattering bells have all one tune,
At weddings, and at funerals: your rich whores
Are only treasuries by extortion fill'd,
And empty'd by curs'd riot. They are worse,   95
Worse than dead bodies, which are begg'd at gallows
And wrought upon by surgeons, to teach man
Wherein he is imperfect. What's a whore?
She's like the guilty counterfeited coin
Which whosoe'er first stamps it brings in trouble   100
All that receive it.

VITTORIA.   This character scapes me.

MONTICELSO. You gentlewoman?
    Take from all beasts, and from all minerals
    Their deadly poison –

VITTORIA.   Well what then?

MONTICELSO.   I'll tell thee –
    I'll find in thee a pothecary's shop   105
    To sample them all.

FRENCH AMBASSADOR. She hath lived ill.

ENGLISH AMBASSADOR. True, but the cardinal's too bitter.

MONTICELSO. You know what whore is – next the devil, Adult'ry,
    Enters the devil, Murder.

FRANCISCO.   Your unhappy
    Husband is dead.

VITTORIA.   O he's a happy husband   110
    Now he owes nature nothing.

FRANCISCO. And by a vaulting engine.

MONTICELSO.   An active plot –
    He jump'd into his grave.

FRANCISCO.   What a prodigy was 't,
    That from some two yards' height a slender man
    Should break his neck?

MONTICELSO.   I' th' rushes.

FRANCISCO.   And what's more,   115
    Upon the instant lose all use of speech,
    All vital motion, like a man had lain
    Wound up three days. Now mark each circumstance.

MONTICELSO. And look upon this creature was his wife.
    She comes not like a widow: she comes arm'd   120
    With scorn and impudence: is this a mourning habit?

VITTORIA. Had I foreknown his death as you suggest,
    I would have bespoke my mourning.

MONTICELSO. O you are cunning.

VITTORIA. You shame your wit and judgement   125
　　To call it so; what, is my just defence
　　By him that is my judge call'd impudence?
　　Let me appeal then from this Christian court
　　To the uncivil Tartar.

MONTICELSO.　　　　　See my lords,
　　She scandals our proceedings.

VITTORIA.　　　　　　　Humbly thus,   130
　　Thus low, to the most worthy and respected
　　Lieger ambassadors, my modesty
　　And womanhood I tender; but withal
　　So entangled in a cursed accusation
　　That my defence of force like Perseus,   135
　　Must personate masculine virtue – to the point!
　　Find me but guilty, sever head from body:
　　We'll part good friends: I scorn to hold my life
　　At yours or any man's entreaty, sir.

ENGLISH AMBASSADOR. She hath a brave spirit.   140

MONTICELSO. Well, well, such counterfeit jewels
　　Make true ones oft suspected.

VITTORIA.　　　　　　　You are deceived;
　　For know that all your strict-combined heads,
　　Which strike against this mine of diamonds,
　　Shall prove but glassen hammers, they shall break, –   145
　　These are but feigned shadows of my evils.
　　Terrify babes, my lord, with painted devils,
　　I am past such needless palsy, – for your names
　　Of whore and murd'ress they proceed from you,
　　As if a man should spit against the wind,   150
　　The filth returns in 's face.

MONTICELSO. Pray you mistress satisfy me one question:
　　Who lodg'd beneath your roof that fatal night
　　Your husband brake his neck?

BRACCIANO.　　　　　　That question
　　Enforceth me break silence, – I was there.   155

MONTICELSO. Your business?

BRACCIANO.   Why I came to comfort her,
  And take some course for settling her estate,
  Because I heard her husband was in debt
  To you my lord.

MONTICELSO.   He was.

BRACCIANO.   And 'twas strangely fear'd
  That you would cozen her.

MONTICELSO.   Who made you overseer?   160

BRACCIANO. Why my charity, my charity, which should flow
  From every generous and noble spirit,
  To orphans and to widows.

MONTICELSO.   Your lust.

BRACCIANO. Cowardly dogs bark loudest. Sirrah priest,
  I'll talk with you hereafter, – Do you hear?   165
  The sword you frame of such an excellent temper,
  I'll sheathe in your own bowels:
  There are a number of thy coat resemble
  Your common post-boys.

MONTICELSO.   Ha?

BRACCIANO.   Your mercenary post-boys, –
  Your letters carry truth, but 'tis your guise   170
  To fill your mouths with gross and impudent lies.

SERVANT. My lord your gown.

BRACCIANO.   Thou liest – 'twas my stool.
  Bestow 't upon thy master that will challenge
  The rest a' th' household stuff – for Bracciano
  Was ne'er so beggarly, to take a stool   175
  Out of another's lodging: let him make
  Valance for his bed on 't, or a demi-foot-cloth
  For his most reverend moil, – Monticelso,
  Nemo me impune lacessit.   179

  Exit BRACCIANO.

MONTICELSO. Your champion's gone.

VITTORIA.   The wolf may prey the better.

FRANCISCO. My lord there's great suspicion of the murder,
　　But no sound proof who did it: for my part
　　I do not think she hath a soul so black
　　To act a deed so bloody, – if she have,
　　As in cold countries husbandmen plant vines,   185
　　And with warm blood manure them, even so
　　One summer she will bear unsavoury fruit,
　　And ere next spring wither both branch and root.
　　The act of blood let pass, only descend
　　To matter of incontinence.

VITTORIA.   I discern poison,   190
　　Under your gilded pills.

MONTICELSO. Now the duke's gone, I will produce a letter,
　　Wherein 'twas plotted he and you should meet,
　　At an apothecary's summer-house,
　　Down by the river Tiber: – view 't my lords: –   195
　　Where after wanton bathing and the heat
　　Of a lascivious banquet . . . I pray read it,
　　I shame to speak the rest.

VITTORIA.   Grant I was tempted,
　　Temptation to lust proves not the act,
　　Casta est quam nemo rogavit, –   200
　　You read his hot love to me, but you want
　　My frosty answer.

MONTICELSO.   Frost i' th' dog-days! strange!

VITTORIA. Condemn you me for that the duke did love me?
　　So may you blame some fair and crystal river
　　For that some melancholic distracted man   205
　　Hath drown'd himself in 't.

MONTICELSO.   Truly drown'd indeed.

VITTORIA. Sum up my faults I pray, and you shall find
　　That beauty and gay clothes, a merry heart,
　　And a good stomach to a feast, are all,

All the poor crimes that you can charge me with: 210
   In faith my lord you might go pistol flies,
   The sport would be more noble.

MONTICELSO.   Very good.

VITTORIA. But take you your course, it seems you have
     beggar'd me first
   And now would fain undo me, – I have houses,
   Jewels, and a poor remnant of crusadoes,   215
   Would those would make you charitable.

MONTICELSO.   If the devil
   Did ever take good shape behold his picture.

VITTORIA. You have one virtue left,
   You will not flatter me.

FRANCISCO.   Who brought this letter?

VITTORIA. I am not compell'd to tell you.   220

MONTICELSO. My lord duke sent to you a thousand ducats,
   The twelfth of August.

VITTORIA.   'Twas to keep your cousin
   From prison, I paid use for 't.

MONTICELSO.   I rather think
   'Twas interest for his lust.

VITTORIA. Who says so but yourself? if you be my accuser   225
   Pray cease to be my judge, come from the bench,
   Give in your evidence 'gainst me, and let these
   Be moderators: my lord cardinal,
   Were your intelligencing ears as long
   As to my thoughts, had you an honest tongue   230
   I would not care though you proclaim'd them all.

MONTICELSO. Go to, go to.
   After your goodly and vain-glorious banquet,
   I'll give you a choke-pear.

VITTORIA.   A' your own grafting?   234

MONTICELSO. You were born in Venice, honourably descended

From the Vitelli; 'twas my cousin's fate, –
Ill may I name the hour – to marry you,
He bought you of your father.

VITTORIA.   Ha?

MONTICELSO. He spent there in six months
　　Twelve thousand ducats, and to my acquaintance   240
　　Receiv'd in dowry with you not one julio:
　　'Twas a hard penny-worth, the ware being so light.
　　I yet but draw the curtain – now to your picture, –
　　You came from thence a most notorious strumpet,
　　And so you have continued.

VITTORIA.   My lord.

MONTICELSO.   Nay hear me,   245
　　You shall have time to prate – my Lord Bracciano, . . .
　　Alas I make but repetition
　　Of what is ordinary and Rialto talk,
　　And ballated, and would be play'd a' th' stage,
　　But that vice many times finds such loud friends   250
　　That preachers are charm'd silent.
　　You gentlemen Flamineo and Marcello,
　　The court hath nothing now to charge you with,
　　Only you must remain upon your sureties
　　For your appearance.

FRANCISCO.   I stand for Marcello.   255

FLAMINEO. And my lord duke for me.

MONTICELSO. For you Vittoria, your public fault,
　　Join'd to th' condition of the present time,
　　Takes from you all the fruits of noble pity.
　　Such a corrupted trial have you made   260
　　Both of your life and beauty, and been styl'd
　　No less in ominous fate than blazing stars
　　To princes; here's your sentence, – you are confin'd
　　Unto a house of convertites and your bawd –   264

FLAMINEO [*aside*]. Who I?

MONTICELSO.   The Moor.

FLAMINEO [*aside*].   O I am a sound man again.

VITTORIA. A house of convertites, what's that?

MONTICELSO.   A house
  Of penitent whores.

VITTORIA.   Do the noblemen in Rome
  Erect it for their wives, that I am sent
  To lodge there?   269

FRANCISCO. You must have patience.

VITTORIA.   I must first have vengeance.
  I fain would know if you have your salvation
  By patent, that you proceed thus.

MONTICELSO.   Away with her.
  Take her hence.

VITTORIA. A rape, a rape.

MONTICELSO.   How?

VITTORIA.   Yes you have ravish'd justice,
  Forc'd her to do your pleasure.

MONTICELSO.   Fie she's mad –   275

VITTORIA. Die with those pills in your most cursed maw,
  Should bring you health, or while you sit a' th' bench,
  Let your own spittle choke you.

MONTICELSO.   She's turn'd Fury.

VITTORIA. That the last day of judgement may so find you,
  And leave you the same devil you were before, –   280
  Instruct me some good horse-leech to speak treason,
  For since you cannot take my life for deeds,
  Take it for words, – O woman's poor revenge
  Which dwells but in the tongue, – I will not weep,
  No I do scorn to call up one poor tear   285
  To fawn on your injustice, – bear me hence,

Unto this house of – what's your mitigating title?

MONTICELSO. Of convertites.

VITTORIA. It shall not be a house of convertites –
    My mind shall make it honester to me   290
    Than the Pope's palace, and more peaceable
    Than thy soul, though thou art a cardinal, –
    Know this, and let it somewhat raise your spite,
    Through darkness diamonds spread their richest light.   294

    Exit VITTORIA [*with* ZANCHE, *guarded*]. *Enter* BRACCIANO.

BRACCIANO. Now you and I are friends sir, we'll shake hands,
    In a friend's grave, together, a fit place,
    Being the emblem of soft peace t' atone our hatred.

FRANCISCO. Sir, what's the matter?

BRACCIANO. I will not chase more blood from that lov'd cheek,
    You have lost too much already, fare-you-well. [*Exit.*]   300

FRANCISCO. How strange these words sound? what's the
    interpretation?

FLAMINEO [*aside*]. Good, this is a preface to the discovery of
    the duchess' death: he carries it well: because now I cannot
    counterfeit a whining passion for the death of my lady, I
    will feign a mad humour for the disgrace of my sister, and   305
    that will keep off idle questions, – treason's tongue hath a
    villainous palsy in 't, I will talk to any man, hear no man,
    and for a time appear a politic madman. [*Exit.*]

    Enter GIOVANNI, *Count* LODOVICO.

FRANCISCO. How now my noble cousin, what in black?

GIOVANNI. Yes uncle, I was taught to imitate you   310
    In virtue, and you must imitate me
    In colours for your garments, – my sweet mother
    Is, . . .

FRANCISCO. How? Where?

GIOVANNI. Is there, – no yonder, – indeed sir I'll not tell you,   315

For I shall make you weep.

FRANCISCO. Is dead.

GIOVANNI. Do not blame me now,
    I did not tell you so.

LODOVICO.   She's dead my lord.

FRANCISCO. Dead?   320

MONTICELSO. Blessed lady; thou art now above thy woes, –
    Will 't please your lordships to withdraw a little?

    [*Exeunt* AMBASSADORS.]

GIOVANNI. What do the dead do, uncle? do they eat,
    Hear music, go a-hunting, and be merry,
    As we that live?   325

FRANCISCO. No coz; they sleep.

GIOVANNI.   Lord, Lord, that I were dead, –
    I have not slept these six nights. When do they wake?

FRANCISCO. When God shall please.

GIOVANNI.   Good God let her sleep ever.
    For I have known her wake an hundred nights,
    When all the pillow, where she laid her head,   330
    Was brine-wet with her tears.
    I am to complain to you sir.
    I'll tell you how they have used her now she's dead:
    They wrapp'd her in a cruel fold of lead,
    And would not let me kiss her.

FRANCISCO.   Thou didst love her.   335

GIOVANNI. I have often heard her say she gave me suck,
    And it should seem by that she dearly lov'd me,
    Since princes seldom do it.

FRANCISCO. O, all of my poor sister that remains!
    Take him away for God's sake.

    [*Exit* GIOVANNI *attended.*]

MONTICELSO.   How now my lord?   340

FRANCISCO. Believe me I am nothing but her grave,
And I shall keep her blessed memory
Longer than thousand epitaphs.

[*Exeunt.*]

Act Three, Scene Three

Enter FLAMINEO *as distracted* [, MARCELLO, *and* LODOVICO].

FLAMINEO. We endure the strokes like anvils or hard steel,
Till pain itself make us no pain to feel.

Who shall do me right now? Is this the end of service?
I'd rather go weed garlic; travail through France, and be
mine own ostler; wear sheep-skin linings; or shoes that   5
stink of blacking; be ent'red into the list of the forty
thousand pedlars in Poland.

Enter SAVOY [AMBASSADOR].

Would I had rotted in some surgeon's house at Venice,
built upon the pox as well as on piles, ere I had serv'd
Bracciano.   10

SAVOY AMBASSADOR. You must have comfort.

FLAMINEO. Your comfortable words are like honey. They
relish well in your mouth that's whole; but in mine that's
wounded they go down as if the sting of the bee were in
them. O they have wrought their purpose cunningly, as if   15
they would not seem to do it of malice. In this a politician
imitates the devil, as the devil imitates a cannon. Where-
soever he comes to do mischief, he comes with his backside
towards you.

Enter the FRENCH [AMBASSADOR].

FRENCH [AMBASSADOR]. The proofs are evident.   20

FLAMINEO. Proof! 'twas corruption. O gold, what a god art

thou! and O man, what a devil art thou to be tempted by
that cursed mineral! Yon diversivolent lawyer; mark him,
knaves turn informers, as maggots turn to flies, – you may
catch gudgeons with either. A cardinal; – I would he   25
would hear me, – there's nothing so holy but money will
corrupt and putrify it, like victual under the line.

Enter ENGLISH AMBASSADOR.

You are happy in England, my lord; here they sell justice
with those weights they press men to death with. O horrible
salary!   30

ENGLISH AMBASSADOR. Fie, fie, Flamineo.

FLAMINEO. Bells ne'er ring well till they are at their full pitch,
and I hope yon cardinal shall never have the grace to pray
well, till he come to the scaffold.

[*Exeunt* AMBASSADORS.]

If they were rack'd now to know the confederacy! But   35
your noblemen are privileged from the rack; and well may.
For a little thing would pull some of them a' pieces ofore
they came to their arraignment. Religion; O how it is
commeddled with policy. The first bloodshed in the
world happened about religion. Would I were a Jew.   40

MARCELLO. O, there are too many.

FLAMINEO. You are deceiv'd. There are not Jews enough;
priests enough, nor gentlemen enough.

MARCELLO. How?

FLAMINEO. I'll prove it. For if there were Jews enough, so   45
many Christians would not turn usurers; if priests enough,
one should not have six benefices; and if gentlemen
enough, so many early mushrooms, whose best growth
sprang from a dunghill, should not aspire to gentility. Farewell. Let others live by begging. Be thou one of them;   50
practise the art of Wolner in England to swallow all's
given thee; and yet let one purgation make thee as hungry
again as fellows that work in a saw-pit. I'll go hear the
screech owl.   54

Exit.

LODOVICO [*aside*]. This was Bracciano's pandar, and 'tis strange
 That in such open and apparent guilt
 Of his adulterous sister, he dare utter
 So scandalous a passion. I must wind him.

 Enter FLAMINEO.

FLAMINEO [*aside*]. How dares this banish'd count return to Rome,
 His pardon not yet purchas'd? I have heard   60
 The deceas'd duchess gave him pension,
 And that he came along from Padua
 I' th' train of the young prince. There's somewhat in 't.
 Physicians, that cure poisons, still do work
 With counterpoisons.

MARCELLO.   Mark this strange encounter.   65

FLAMINEO. The god of melancholy turn thy gall to poison,
 And let the stigmatic wrinkles in thy face,
 Like to the boisterous waves in a rough tide,
 One still overtake another.

LODOVICO.   I do thank thee
 And I do wish ingeniously for thy sake   70
 The dog-days all year long.

FLAMINEO.   How croaks the raven?
 Is our good duchess dead?

LODOVICO.   Dead –

FLAMINEO.   O fate!
 Misfortune comes like the coroner's business,
 Huddle upon huddle.

LODOVICO. Shalt thou and I join housekeeping?

FLAMINEO.   Yes, content. 75
 Let's be unsociably sociable.

LODOVICO. Sit some three days together, and discourse.

FLAMINEO. Only with making faces;
 Lie in our clothes.

LODOVICO. With faggots for our pillows.

FLAMINEO.   And be lousy.   80

LODOVICO. In taffeta linings; that's gentle melancholy, –
   Sleep all day.

FLAMINEO.   Yes: and like your melancholic hare
   Feed after midnight.

   Enter ANTONELLI [*and* GASPARO, *laughing*].

   We are observed: see how yon couple grieve.

LODOVICO. What a strange creature is a laughing fool,   85
   As if man were created to no use
   But only to show his teeth.

FLAMINEO.   I'll tell thee what, –
   It would do well instead of looking-glasses
   To set one's face each morning by a saucer
   Of a witch's congealed blood.

LODOVICO..   Precious girn, rogue.   90
   We'll never part.

FLAMINEO. Never: till the beggary of courtiers,
   The discontent of churchmen, want of soldiers,
   And all the creatures that hang manacled,
   Worse than strappado'd, on the lowest felly   95
   Of Fortune's wheel be taught in our two lives
   To scorn that world which life of means deprives.

ANTONELLI. My lord, I bring good news. The Pope
      on 's death-bed,
   At th' earnest suit of the great Duke of Florence,
   Hath sign'd your pardon, and restor'd unto you –   100

LODOVICO. I thank you for your news. Look up again
   Flamineo, see my pardon.

FLAMINEO.   Why do you laugh?
   There was no such condition in our covenant.

LODOVICO. Why?

FLAMINEO. You shall not seem a happier man than I, –   105

You know our vow sir, if you will be merry,
Do it i' th' like posture, as if some great man
Sate while his enemy were executed:
Though it be very lechery unto thee,
Do't with a crabbed politician's face.   110

LODOVICO. Your sister is a damnable whore.

FLAMINEO.   Ha?

LODOVICO. Look you; I spake that laughing.

FLAMINEO. Dost ever think to speak again?

LODOVICO.   Do you hear?
Wilt sell me forty ounces of her blood,
To water a mandrake?

FLAMINEO.   Poor lord, you did vow   115
To live a lousy creature.

LODOVICO.   Yes; –

FLAMINEO.   Like one
That had for ever forfeited the daylight,
By being in debt, –

LODOVICO.   Ha, ha!

FLAMINEO. I do not greatly wonder you do break:
Your lordship learnt long since. But I'll tell you, –   120

LODOVICO. What?

FLAMINEO.   And 't shall stick by you.

LODOVICO.   I long for it.

FLAMINEO. This laughter scurvily becomes your face, –
If you will not be melancholy, be angry.

Strikes him.

See, now I laugh too.   124

MARCELLO. You are to blame, I'll force you hence.

LODOVICO.   Unhand me:

Exit MARCELLO and FLAMINEO.

That e'er I should be forc'd to right myself,
Upon a pandar.

ANTONELLI.   My lord.

LODOVICO. H' had been as good met with his fist a thunderbolt.

GASPARO. How this shows!

LODOVICO.   Ud's death, how did my sword miss him?
These rogues that are most weary of their lives,   130
Still scape the greatest dangers, . . .
A pox upon him: all his reputation; –
Nay all the goodness of his family; –
Is not worth half this earthquake.
I learnt it of no fencer to shake thus;   135
Come I'll forget him, and go drink some wine.

Exeunt.

Act Four, Scene One

Enter FRANCISCO *and* MONTICELSO.

MONTICELSO. Come, come my lord, untie your folded thoughts,
And let them dangle loose as a bride's hair.
Your sister's poisoned.

FRANCISCO.   Far be it from my thoughts
To seek revenge.

MONTICELSO.   What, are you turn'd all marble?

FRANCISCO. Shall I defy him, and impose a war   5
Most burdensome on my poor subjects' necks,
Which at my will I have not power to end?
You know: for all the murders, rapes, and thefts,
Committed in the horrid lust of war,
He that unjustly caus'd it first proceed,   10
Shall find it in his grave and in his seed.

MONTICELSO. That's not the course I'd wish you: pray,
     observe me, –
We see that undermining more prevails
Than doth the cannon. Bear your wrongs conceal'd,
And, patient as the tortoise, let this camel   15
Stalk o'er your back unbruis'd: sleep with the lion,
And let this brood of secure foolish mice
Play with your nostrils, till the time be ripe
For th' bloody audit, and the fatal gripe:
Aim like a cunning fowler, close one eye,   20
That you the better may your game espy.

FRANCISCO. Free me my innocence, from treacherous acts:
I know there's thunder yonder: and I'll stand,
Like a safe valley, which low bends the knee
To some aspiring mountain: since I know   25

Treason, like spiders weaving nets for flies,
By her foul work is found, and in it dies.
To pass away these thoughts, my honour'd lord,
It is reported you possess a book
Wherein you have quoted, by intelligence,   30
The names of all notorious offenders
Lurking about the city, –

MONTICELSO.   Sir I do;
And some there are which call it my black book:
Well may the title hold: for though it teach not
The art of conjuring, yet in it lurk   35
The names of many devils.

FRANCISCO.   Pray let's see it.

MONTICELSO. I'll fetch it to your lordship.

    Exit MONTICELSO.

FRANCISCO.   Monticelso,
I will not trust thee, but in all my plots
I'll rest as jealous as a town besieg'd.
Thou canst not reach what I intend to act;   40
Your flax soon kindles, soon is out again,
But gold slow heats, and long will hot remain.

    [*Re-*]*enter* MONTICELSO; *presents* FRANCISCO *with a book.*

MONTICELSO. 'Tis here my lord.

FRANCISCO. First your intelligencers – pray let's see.

MONTICELSO. Their number rises strangely,   45
And some of them
You'd take for honest men.
Next are panders.
These are your pirates: and these following leaves,
For base rogues that undo young gentlemen   50
By taking up commodities:
For politic bankrupts:
For fellows that are bawds to their own wives,
Only to put off horses and slight jewels,
Clocks, defac'd plate, and such commodities,   55

At birth of their first children.

FRANCISCO.   Are there such?

MONTICELSO. These are for impudent bawds,
    That go in men's apparel: for usurers
    That share with scriveners for their good reportage:
    For lawyers that will antedate their writs: 60
    And some divines you might find folded there,
    But that I slip them o'er for conscience' sake.
    Here is a general catalogue of knaves.
    A man might study all the prisons o'er,
    Yet never attain this knowledge.

FRANCISCO.   Murderers.   65
    Fold down the leaf I pray, –
    Good my lord let me borrow this strange doctrine.

MONTICELSO. Pray use 't my lord.

FRANCISCO.   I do assure your lordship,
    You are a worthy member of the state,
    And have done infinite good in your discovery   70
    Of these offenders.

MONTICELSO.   Somewhat sir.

FRANCISCO.   O God!
    Better than tribute of wolves paid in England;
    'Twill hang their skins o' th' hedge.

MONTICELSO.   I must make bold
    To leave your lordship.

FRANCISCO.   Dearly sir, I thank you, –
    If any ask for me at court, report   75
    You have left me in the company of knaves.

Exit MONTICELSO.

I gather now by this, some cunning fellow
That's my lord's officer, one that lately skipp'd
From a clerk's desk up to a justice' chair,
Hath made this knavish summons; and intends,   80
As th' Irish rebels wont were to sell heads,

So to make prize of these. And thus it happens,
Your poor rogues pay for 't, which have not the means
To present bribe in fist: the rest o' th' band
Are raz'd out of the knaves' record; or else   85
My lord he winks at them with easy will,
His man grows rich, the knaves are the knaves still.
But to the use I'll make of it; it shall serve
To point me out a list of murderers,
Agents for any villainy. Did I want   90
Ten leash of courtezans, it would furnish me;
Nay laundress three armies. That in so little paper
Should lie th' undoing of so many men!
'Tis not so big as twenty declarations.
See the corrupted use some make of books: 95
Divinity, wrested by some factious blood,
Draws swords, swells battles, and o'erthrows all good.
To fashion my revenge more seriously,
Let me remember my dead sister's face:
Call for her picture: no, I'll close mine eyes,   100
And in a melancholic thought I'll frame
Her figure 'fore me.

Enter ISABELLA's *Ghost.*

                            Now I ha 't – how strong
Imagination works! how she can frame
Things which are not! methinks she stands afore me;
And by the quick idea of my mind,   105
Were my skill pregnant, I could draw her picture.
Thought, as a subtle juggler, makes us deem
Things supernatural, which have cause
Common as sickness. 'Tis my melancholy, –
How cam'st thou by thy death? – how idle am I   110
To question mine own idleness? – did ever
Man dream awake till now? – remove this object –
Out of my brain with 't: what have I to do
With tombs, or death-beds, funerals, or tears,
That have to meditate upon revenge?   115

[*Exit* GHOST.]

So now 'tis ended, like an old wives' story.
Statesmen think often they see stranger sights
Than madmen. Come, to this weighty business.
My tragedy must have some idle mirth in 't,
Else it will never pass. I am in love,   120
In love with Corombona; and my suit
Thus halts to her in verse. –

He writes.

I have done it rarely: O the fate of princes!
I am so us'd to frequent flattery,
That being alone I now flatter myself;   125
But it will serve, 'tis seal'd;

Enter SERVANT.
                                   bear this
To th' house of convertites; and watch your leisure
To give it to the hands of Corombona,
Or to the matron, when some followers
Of Bracciano may be by. Away –   130

Exit SERVANT.

He that deals all by strength, his wit is shallow:
When a man's head goes through each limb will follow.
The engine for my business, bold Count Lodowick: –
'Tis gold must such an instrument procure,
With empty fist no man doth falcons lure.   135
Bracciano, I am now fit for thy encounter.
Like the wild Irish I'll ne'er think thee dead,
Till I can play at football with thy head.
Flectere si nequeo superos, Acheronta movebo.

Exit.

Act Four, Scene Two

Enter the MATRON, *and* FLAMINEO.

MATRON. Should it be known the duke hath such recourse

To your imprison'd sister, I were like
T' incur much damage by it.

FLAMINEO.   Not a scruple.
The Pope lies on his death-bed, and their heads
Are troubled now with other business   5
Than guarding of a lady.

Enter SERVANT.

SERVANT [*aside*]. Yonder's Flamineo in conference
With the matrona. [*To the* MATRON.] Let me speak with you.
I would entreat you to deliver for me
This letter to the fair Vittoria.   10

MATRON. I shall sir.

Enter BRACCIANO.

SERVANT.   With all care and secrecy, –
Hereafter you shall know me, and receive
Thanks for this courtesy. [*Exit.*]

FLAMINEO.   How now? what's that?

MATRON. A letter.

FLAMINEO.   To my sister: I'll see 't delivered.

[*Exit* MATRON.]

BRACCIANO. What's that you read Flamineo?

FLAMINEO.   Look.   15

BRACCIANO. Ha? [*Reads.*] *'To the most unfortunate his best respected*
Vittoria' –

Who was the messenger?

FLAMINEO.   I know not.

BRACCIANO. No! Who sent it?

FLAMINEO.   Ud's foot you speak, as if a man
Should know what fowl is coffin'd in a bak'd meat   20
Afore you cut it up.

BRACCIANO. I'll open 't, were 't her heart. What's here subscribed –

'Florence'? This juggling is gross and palpable.
I have found out the conveyance; read it, read it.   24

FLAMINEO [*reads*]. *'Your tears I'll turn to triumphs, be but mine.*
Your prop is fall'n; I pity that a vine
Which princes heretofore have long'd to gather,
Wanting supporters, now should fade and wither.'
Wine i' faith, my lord, with lees would serve his turn.
'Your sad imprisonment I'll soon uncharm,   30
And with a princely uncontrolled arm
Lead you to Florence, where my love and care
Shall hang your wishes in my silver hair.'
A halter on his strange equivocation!
'Nor for my years return me the sad willow, –   35
Who prefer blossoms before fruit that's mellow?'
Rotten on my knowledge with lying too long i' th' bed-straw.
'And all the lines of age this line convinces:
The gods never wax old, no more do princes.'
A pox on 't – tear it, let's have no more atheists for God's sake. 40

BRACCIANO. Ud's death, I'll cut her into atomies
And let th' irregular north-wind sweep her up
And blow her int' his nostrils. Where's this whore?

FLAMINEO. That – ? what do you call her?

BRACCIANO.   O, I could be mad;   45
Prevent the curst disease she'll bring me to,
And tear my hair off. Where's this changeable stuff?

FLAMINEO. O'er head and ears in water, I assure you, –
She is not for your wearing.

BRACCIANO.   In you pander!

FLAMINEO. What me, my lord, am I your dog?   50

BRACCIANO. A blood-hound: do you brave? do you stand me?

FLAMINEO. Stand you? let those that have diseases run;
I need no plasters.

BRACCIANO. Would you be kick'd?

FLAMINEO.   Would you have your neck broke?

I tell you duke, I am not in Russia;   55
My shins must be kept whole.

BRACCIANO.   Do you know me?

FLAMINEO. O my lord! methodically.
    As in this world there are degrees of evils:
    So in this world there are degrees of devils.
    You're a great duke; I your poor secretary.   60
    I do look now for a Spanish fig, or an Italian sallet daily.

BRACCIANO. Pander, ply your convoy, and leave your prating.

FLAMINEO. All your kindness to me is like that miserable
    courtesy of Polyphemus to Ulysses, – you reserve me to be
    devour'd last, – you would dig turves out of my grave to   65
    feed your larks: that would be music to you. Come, I'll lead
    you to her.

BRACCIANO. Do you face me?

FLAMINEO. O sir I would not go before a politic enemy with
    my back towards him, though there were behind me a whirl-   70
    pool.

Enter VITTORIA *to* BRACCIANO *and* FLAMINEO.

BRACCIANO. Can you read mistress? look upon that letter;
    There are no characters nor hieroglyphics.
    You need no comment, I am grown your receiver, –
    God's precious, you shall be a brave great lady,   75
    A stately and advanced whore.

VITTORIA.   Say sir?

BRACCIANO. Come, come, let's see your cabinet, discover
    Your treasury of love-letters. Death and furies,
    I'll see them all.

VITTORIA.   Sir, upon my soul,
    I have not any. Whence was this directed?   80

BRACCIANO. Confusion on your politic ignorance!

    [*Gives her the letter.*]

    You are reclaimed, are you? I'll give you the bells

And let you fly to the devil.

FLAMINEO.   Ware hawk, my lord.

VITTORIA. *'Florence'!* This is some treacherous plot, my lord, –
To me, he ne'er was lovely I protest,   85
So much as in my sleep.

BRACCIANO.   Right: they are plots.
Your beauty! O, ten thousand curses on 't.
How long have I beheld the devil in crystal?
Thou hast led me, like an heathen sacrifice,
With music, and with fatal yokes of flowers   90
To my eternal ruin. Woman to man
Is either a god or a wolf.

VITTORIA.   My lord.

BRACCIANO.   Away.
We'll be as differing as two adamants;
The one shall shun the other. What? dost weep?
Procure but ten of thy dissembling trade,   95
Ye'd furnish all the Irish funerals
With howling, past wild Irish.

FLAMINEO.   Fie, my lord.

BRACCIANO. That hand, that cursed hand, which I have wearied
With doting kisses! O my sweetest duchess   99
How lovely art thou now! [*To* VITTORIA.] Thy loose thoughts
Scatter like quicksilver, I was bewitch'd;
For all the world speaks ill of thee.

VITTORIA.   No matter.
I'll live so now I'll make that world recant
And change her speeches. You did name your duchess.   104

BRACCIANO. Whose death God pardon.

VITTORIA.   Whose death God revenge
On thee most godless duke.

FLAMINEO.   Now for two whirlwinds.

VITTORIA. What have I gain'd by thee but infamy?
Thou hast stain'd the spotless honour of my house,

And frighted thence noble society:
Like those, which sick o' th' palsy, and retain   110
Ill-scenting foxes 'bout them, are still shunn'd
By those of choicer nostrils.
What do you call this house?
Is this your palace? did not the judge style it
A house of penitent whores? who sent me to it?   115
Who hath the honour to advance Vittoria
To this incontinent college? is 't not you?
Is 't not your high preferment? Go, go brag
How many ladies you have undone, like me.
Fare you well sir; let me hear no more of you.   120
I had a limb corrupted to an ulcer,
But I have cut it off: and now I'll go
Weeping to heaven on crutches. For your gifts,
I will return them all; and I do wish
That I could make you full executor   125
To all my sins, – O that I could toss myself
Into a grave as quickly: for all thou art worth
I'll not shed one tear more; – I'll burst first.

She throws herself upon a bed.

BRACCIANO. I have drunk Lethe. Vittoria?
My dearest happiness? Vittoria?   130
What do you ail my love? why do you weep?

VITTORIA. Yes, I now weep poniards, do you see?

BRACCIANO. Are not those matchless eyes mine?

VITTORIA.   I had rather
They were not matches.

BRACCIANO.   Is not this lip mine?

VITTORIA. Yes: thus to bite it off, rather than give it thee.   135

FLAMINEO. Turn to my lord, good sister.

VITTORIA.   Hence you pander.

FLAMINEO. Pander! Am I the author of your sin?

VITTORIA. Yes: he's a base thief that a thief lets in.

FLAMINEO. We're blown up, my lord, –

BRACCIANO.   Wilt thou hear me?
    Once to be jealous of thee is t' express   140
    That I will love thee everlastingly,
    And never more be jealous.

VITTORIA.   O thou fool,
    Whose greatness hath by much o'ergrown thy wit!
    What dar'st thou do, that I not dare to suffer,
    Excepting to be still thy whore? for that,   145
    In the sea's bottom sooner thou shalt make
    A bonfire.

FLAMINEO. O, no oaths for God's sake.

BRACCIANO. Will you hear me?

VITTORIA.   Never.

FLAMINEO. What a damn'd imposthume is a woman's will?
    Can nothing break it? fie, fie, my lord.   150
    [*Aside to* BRACCIANO.] Women are caught as you take tortoises,
    She must be turn'd on her back. [*Aloud.*] Sister, by this hand
    I am on your side. Come, come, you have wrong'd her.
    What a strange credulous man were you, my lord,
    To think the Duke of Florence would love her?   155
    [*Aside.*] Will any mercer take another's ware
    When once 'tis tous'd and sullied? [*Aloud.*] And, yet sister,
    How scurvily this frowardness becomes you!
    [*Aside.*] Young leverets stand not long; and women's anger
    Should, like their flight, procure a little sport;   160
    A full cry for a quarter of an hour,
    And then be put to th' dead quat.

BRACCIANO.   Shall these eyes,
    Which have so long time dwelt upon your face,
    Be now put out?

FLAMINEO. No cruel landlady i' th' world, which lends forth   165
    groats to broom-men, and takes use for them, would do't.

    [*Aside to* BRACCIANO.] Hand her, my lord, and kiss her: be not
    like

A ferret to let go your hold with blowing.

BRACCIANO. Let us renew right hands.

VITTORIA. Hence.

BRACCIANO. Never shall rage, or the forgetful wine, 170
    Make me commit like fault.

FLAMINEO [*aside to* BRACCIANO]. Now you are i' th' way on 't,
    follow 't hard.

BRACCIANO. Be thou at peace with me; let all the world
    Threaten the cannon.

FLAMINEO. Mark his penitence.
    Best natures do commit the grossest faults,175
    When they're giv'n o'er to jealousy; as best wine
    Dying makes strongest vinegar. I'll tell you;
    The sea's more rough and raging than calm rivers,
    But nor so sweet nor wholesome. A quiet woman
    Is a still water under a great bridge.180
    A man may shoot her safely.

VITTORIA. O ye dissembling men!

FLAMINEO. We suck'd that, sister,
    From women's breasts, in our first infancy.

VITTORIA. To add misery to misery.

BRACCIANO. Sweetest.

VITTORIA. Am I not low enough?185
    Ay, ay, your good heart gathers like a snowball
    Now your affection's cold.

FLAMINEO. Ud's foot, it shall melt
    To a heart again, or all the wine in Rome
    Shall run o' th' lees for 't.

VITTORIA. Your dog or hawk should be rewarded better190
    Than I have been. I'll speak not one word more.

FLAMINEO. Stop her mouth,
    With a sweet kiss, my lord.
    So now the tide's turned the vessel's come about –

He's a sweet armful. O we curl'd-hair'd men   195
Are still most kind to women. This is well.

BRACCIANO. That you should chide thus!

FLAMINEO.   O, sir, your little chimneys
Do ever cast most smoke. I sweat for you.
Couple together with as deep a silence
As did the Grecians in their wooden horse.   200
My lord supply your promises with deeds;
You know that painted meat no hunger feeds.

BRACCIANO. Stay – ingrateful Rome!

FLAMINEO. Rome! it deserves to be call'd Barbary, for our
villainous usage.   205

BRACCIANO. Soft; the same project which the Duke of Florence,
(Whether in love or gullery I know not)
Laid down for her escape, will I pursue.

FLAMINEO. And no time fitter than this night, my lord;
The Pope being dead; and all the cardinals ent'red   210
The conclave for th' electing a new Pope;
The city in a great confusion;
We may attire her in a page's suit,
Lay her post-horse, take shipping, and amain
For Padua.   215

BRACCIANO. I'll instantly steal forth the Prince Giovanni,
And make for Padua. You two with your old mother
And young Marcello that attends on Florence,
If you can work him to it, follow me.
I will advance you all: for you Vittoria,   220
Think of a duchess' title.

FLAMINEO.   Lo you sister.

Stay, my lord; I'll tell you a tale. The crocodile, which
lives in the river Nilus, hath a worm breeds i' th' teeth of 't,
which puts it to extreme anguish: a little bird, no bigger
than a wren, is barber-surgeon to this crocodile; flies into   225
the jaws of 't; picks out the worm; and brings present
remedy. The fish, glad of ease but ingrateful to her that

did it, that the bird may not talk largely of her abroad for
non-payment, closeth her chaps intending to swallow her,
and so put her to perpetual silence. But nature loathing   230
such ingratitude, hath arm'd this bird with a quill
or prick on the head, top o' th' which wounds the
crocodile i' th' mouth; forceth her open her bloody
prison; and away flies the pretty tooth-picker from her
cruel patient.   235

BRACCIANO. Your application is, I have not rewarded
    The service you have done me.

FLAMINEO.   No, my lord;

You sister are the crocodile: you are blemish'd in your
fame, my lord cures it. And though the comparison hold
not in every particle, yet observe, remember, what good   240
the bird with the prick i' th' head hath done you; and
scorn ingratitude.

[*Aside.*] It may appear to some ridiculous
Thus to talk knave and madman; and sometimes
Come in with a dried sentence, stuff'd with sage.   245
But this allows my varying of shapes, –
Knaves do grow great by being great men's apes.

Exeunt.

Act Four, Scene Three

Enter LODOVICO, GASPARO, *and six* AMBASSADORS.
At another door [FRANCISCO] *the Duke of Florence.*

FRANCISCO. So, my lord, I commend your diligence –
    Guard well the conclave, and, as the order is,
    Let none have conference with the cardinals.

LODOVICO. I shall, my lord: room for the ambassadors, –

GASPARO. They're wondrous brave today: why do they wear   5
    These several habits?

LODOVICO.   O sir, they're knights
  Of several orders.
  That lord i' th' black cloak with the silver cross
  Is Knight of Rhodes; the next Knight of S. Michael;
  That of the Golden Fleece; the Frenchman there   10
  Knight of the Holy Ghost; my lord of Savoy
  Knight of th' Annunciation; the Englishman
  Is Knight of th' honoured Garter, dedicated
  Unto their saint, S. George. I could describe to you
  Their several institutions, with the laws   15
  Annexed to their orders; but that time
  Permits not such discovery.

FRANCISCO.   Where's Count Lodowick?

LODOVICO. Here my lord.

FRANCISCO.   'Tis o' th' point of dinner time,
  Marshal the cardinals' service, –

LODOVICO.   Sir I shall.

Enter SERVANTS *with several dishes covered.*

  Stand, let me search your dish, – who's this for?   20

SERVANT. For my Lord Cardinal Monticelso.

LODOVICO. Whose this?

SERVANT.   For my Lord Cardinal of Bourbon.

FRENCH AMBASSADOR. Why doth he search the dishes? –
  to observe
  What meat is dress'd?

ENGLISH AMBASSADOR. No sir, but to prevent
  Lest any letters should be convey'd in   25
  To bribe or to solicit the advancement
  Of any cardinal, – when first they enter
  'Tis lawful for the ambassadors of princes
  To enter with them, and to make their suit
  For any man their prince affecteth best;   30
  But after, till a general election,
  No man may speak with them.

LODOVICO. You that attend on the lord cardinals
  Open the window, and receive their viands.

  [*A* CONCLAVIST *appears briefly at the window.*]

CONCLAVIST. You must return the service; the lord cardinals   35
  Are busied 'bout electing of the Pope, –
  They have given o'er scrutiny, and are fallen
  To admiration.

LODOVICO.   Away, away.

FRANCISCO. I'll lay a thousand ducats you hear news
  Of a Pope presently, – hark; sure he's elected, –   40

  [*The*] *Cardinal* [*of* ARRAGON *appears*] *on the terrace.*
  Behold! my lord of Arragon appears
  On the church battlements.

ARRAGON. *Denuntio vobis gaudium magnum. Reverendissimus*
  Cardinalis Lorenzo de Monticelso electus est in sedem apostoli-
  cam, et elegit sibi nomen Paulum Quartum.   45

OMNES. *Vivat Sanctus Pater Paulus Quartus.*

  [*Enter* SERVANT.]

SERVANT. Vittoria my lord –

FRANCISCO.   Well: what of her?

SERVANT. Is fled the city, –

FRANCISCO.   Ha?

SERVANT.   With Duke Bracciano.

FRANCISCO. Fled? Where's the prince Giovanni?

SERVANT.   Gone with his father.

FRANCISCO. Let the matrona of the convertites   50
  Be apprehended: fled – O damnable!

  [*Exit* SERVANT.]

  [*Aside.*] How fortunate are my wishes. Why? 'twas this
  I only laboured. I did send the letter
  T' instruct him what to do. Thy fame, fond duke,

I first have poison'd; directed thee the way   55
To marry a whore; what can be worse? This follows:
The hand must act to drown the passionate tongue, –
I scorn to wear a sword and prate of wrong.

Enter MONTICELSO *in state.*

MONTICELSO. *Concedimus vobis apostolicam benedictionem*
    et remissionem peccatorum.   60

[FRANCISCO *whispers to him.*]

My lord reports Vittoria Corombona
Is stol'n from forth the house of convertites
By Bracciano, and they're fled the city.
Now, though this be the first day of our seat,
We cannot better please the divine power,   65
Than to sequester from the holy church
These cursed persons. Make it therefore known,
We do denounce excommunication
Against them both: all that are theirs in Rome
We likewise banish. Set on.   70

Exeunt [*all except* FRANCISCO *and* LODOVICO].

FRANCISCO. Come dear Lodovico.
    You have ta'en the sacrament to prosecute
    Th' intended murder.

LODOVICO.   With all constancy.
    But, sir, I wonder you'll engage yourself,
    In person, being a great prince.

FRANCISCO.   Divert me not.   75
    Most of his court are of my faction,
    And some are of my counsel. Noble friend,
    Our danger shall be 'like in this design, –
    Give leave, part of the glory may be mine.

Exit FRANCISCO. [*Re-*]*enter* MONTICELSO.

MONTICELSO. Why did the Duke of Florence with such care   80
    Labour your pardon? say.

LODOVICO. Italian beggars will resolve you that

Who, begging of an alms, bid those they beg of
Do good for their own sakes; or 't may be
He spreads his bounty with a sowing hand,   85
Like kings, who many times give out of measure;
Not for desert so much as for their pleasure.

MONTICELSO. I know you're cunning. Come, what devil was that
    That you were raising?

LODOVICO.   Devil, my lord?

MONTICELSO.   I ask you
    How doth the duke employ you, that his bonnet   90
    Fell with such compliment unto his knee,
    When he departed from you?

LODOVICO.   Why, my lord,
    He told me of a resty Barbary horse
    Which he would fain have brought to the career,
    The 'sault, and the ring-galliard. Now, my lord,   95
    I have a rare French rider.

MONTICELSO.   Take you heed:
    Lest the jade break your neck. Do you put me off
    With your wild horse-tricks? Sirrah you do lie.
    O, thou 'rt a foul black cloud, and thou dost threat
    A violent storm.

LODOVICO.   Storms are i' th' air, my lord;   100
    I am too low to storm.

MONTICELSO.   Wretched creature!
    I know that thou art fashion'd for all ill,
    Like dogs, that once get blood, they'll ever kill.
    About some murder? was 't not?

LODOVICO.   I'll not tell you;
    And yet I care not greatly if I do;   105
    Marry with this preparation. Holy father,
    I come not to you as an intelligencer,
    But as a penitent sinner. What I utter
    Is in confession merely; which you know

Must never be reveal'd.

MONTICELSO.   You have o'erta'en me.   110

LODOVICO. Sir I did love Bracciano's duchess dearly;
   Or rather I pursued her with hot lust,
   Though she ne'er knew on 't. She was poison'd;
   Upon my soul she was: for which I have sworn
   T' avenge her murder.

MONTICELSO.   To the Duke of Florence?   115

LODOVICO. To him I have.

MONTICELSO.   Miserable creature!
   If thou persist in this, 'tis damnable.
   Dost thou imagine thou canst slide on blood
   And not be tainted with a shameful fall?
   Or like the black, and melancholic yew tree,   120
   Dost think to root thyself in dead men's graves,
   And yet to prosper? Instruction to thee
   Comes like sweet showers to over-hard'ned ground:
   They wet, but pierce not deep. And so I leave thee
   With all the Furies hanging 'bout thy neck,   125
   Till by thy penitence thou remove this evil,
   In conjuring from thy breast that cruel devil.

   Exit MONTICELSO.

LODOVICO. I'll give it o'er. He says 'tis damnable:
   Besides I did expect his suffrage,
   By reason of Camillo's death.   130

   Enter SERVANT *and* FRANCISCO [*and stand aside*].

FRANCISCO. Do you know that count?

SERVANT.   Yes, my lord.

FRANCISCO. Bear him these thousand ducats to his lodging;
   Tell him the Pope hath sent them. Happily
   That will confirm more than all the rest.

   [*Exit.*]

SERVANT. Sir.   135

LODOVICO. To me sir?

SERVANT. His Holiness hath sent you a thousand crowns,
    And wills you if you travail, to make him
    Your patron for intelligence.

LODOVICO.   His creature
    Ever to be commanded. [*Exit* SERVANT.]   140
    Why now 'tis come about. He rail'd upon me;
    And yet these crowns were told out and laid ready,
    Before he knew my voyage. O the art,
    The modest form of greatness! that do sit
    Like brides at wedding dinners, with their looks turn'd   145
    From the least wanton jests, their puling stomach
    Sick of the modesty, when their thoughts are loose,
    Even acting of those hot and lustful sports
    Are to ensue about midnight: such his cunning!
    He sounds my depth thus with a golden plummet, –   150
    I am doubly arm'd now. Now to th' act of blood;
    There's but three Furies found in spacious hell,
    But in a great man's breast three thousand dwell.

    [*Exit.*]

Act Five, Scene One

A passage over the stage of BRACCIANO, FLAMINEO, MARCELLO, HORTENSIO, [VITTORIA] COROMBONA, CORNELIA, ZANCHE *and others.* [FLAMINEO *and* HORTENSIO *remain.*]

FLAMINEO. In all the weary minutes of my life,
    Day ne'er broke up till now. This marriage
    Confirms me happy.

HORTENSIO.   'Tis a good assurance.
    Saw you not yet the Moor that's come to court?

FLAMINEO. Yes, and conferr'd with him i' th' duke's closet, –   5
    I have not seen a goodlier personage,
    Nor ever talk'd with man better experienc'd
    In state affairs or rudiments of war.
    He hath by report, serv'd the Venetian
    In Candy these twice seven years, and been chief   10
    In many a bold design.

HORTENSIO.   What are those two
    That bear him company?

FLAMINEO. Two noblemen of Hungary, that living in the
    emperor's service as commanders, eight years since, contrary
    to the expectation of all the court ent'red into religion,   15
    into the strict order of Capuchins: but being not well settled
    in their undertaking they left their order and returned to
    court: for which being after troubled in conscience, they
    vowed their service against the enemies of Christ; went to
    Malta; were there knighted; and in their return back, at   20
    this great solemnity, they are resolved for ever to forsake
    the world, and settle themselves here in a house of
    Capuchins in Padua.

HORTENSIO. 'Tis strange.

FLAMINEO. One thing makes it so. They have vowed for 25
    ever to wear next their bare bodies those coats of mail
    they served in.

HORTENSIO. Hard penance. Is the Moor a Christian?

FLAMINEO. He is.

HORTENSIO. Why proffers he his service to our duke? 30

FLAMINEO. Because he understands there's like to grow
    Some wars between us and the Duke of Florence,
    In which he hopes employment.
    I never saw one in a stern bold look
    Wear more command, nor in a lofty phrase 35
    Express more knowing, or more deep contempt
    Of our slight airy courtiers. He talks
    As if he had travail'd all the princes' courts
    Of Christendom; in all things strives t' express
    That all that should dispute with him may know 40
    Glories, like glow-worms, afar off shine bright
    But look'd to near, have neither heat nor light.
    The duke!

Enter BRACCIANO, [FRANCISCO *Duke of*] *Florence disguised*
like Mulinassar; LODOVICO, ANTONELLI, [*and*] GASPARO
[*disguised, and another*], *bearing their swords and helmets*[, CARLO
and PEDRO].

BRACCIANO. You are nobly welcome. We have heard at full
    Your honourable service 'gainst the Turk. 45
    To you, brave Mulinassar, we assign
    A competent pension: and are inly sorrow
    The vows of these two worthy gentlemen
    Make them incapable of our proffer'd bounty.
    Your wish is you may leave your warlike swords 50
    For monuments in our chapel. I accept it
    As a great honour done me, and must crave
    Your leave to furnish out our duchess' revels.
    Only one thing, as the last vanity
    You e'er shall view, deny me not to stay 55
    To see a barriers prepar'd tonight;

You shall have private standings: it hath pleas'd
The great ambassadors of several princes
In their return from Rome to their own countries
To grace our marriage, and to honour me   60
With such a kind of sport.

FRANCISCO.   I shall persuade them
To stay, my lord.

BRACCIANO.   Set on there to the presence.

Exeunt BRACCIANO, FLAMINEO, *and* [HORTENSIO].

CARLO. Noble my lord, most fortunately welcome,

The conspirators here embrace.

You have our vows seal'd with the sacrament
To second your attempts.

PEDRO.   And all things ready.   65
He could not have invented his own ruin,
Had he despair'd, with more propriety.

LODOVICO. You would not take my way.

FRANCISCO.   'Tis better ordered.

LODOVICO. T' have poison'd his prayer book, or a pair of beads,
The pommel of his saddle, his looking-glass,   70
Or th' handle of his racket, – O that, that!
That while he had been bandying at tennis,
He might have sworn himself to hell, and struck
His soul into the hazard! O my lord!
I would have our plot be ingenious,   75
And have it hereafter recorded for example
Rather than borrow example.

FRANCISCO.   There's no way
More speeding than this thought on.

LODOVICO.   On then.

FRANCISCO. And yet methinks that this revenge is poor,
Because it steals upon him like a thief, –   80
To have ta'en him by the casque in a pitch'd field,

Led him to Florence!

LODOVICO.   It had been rare. – And there
　　Have crown'd him with a wreath of stinking garlic,
　　T' have shown the sharpness of his government,
　　And rankness of his lust. Flamineo comes.   85

　　Exeunt [all except FRANCISCO]. *Enter* FLAMINEO,
　　MARCELLO, *and* ZANCHE.

MARCELLO. Why doth this devil haunt you? say.

FLAMINEO.   I know not.
　　For by this light I do not conjure for her.
　　'Tis not so great a cunning as men think
　　To raise the devil: for here's one up already, –
　　The greatest cunning were to lay him down –   90

MARCELLO. She is your shame.

FLAMINEO.   I prithee pardon her.
　　In faith you see, women are like to burs;
　　Where their affection throws them, there they'll stick.

ZANCHE. That is my countryman, a goodly person;
　　When he's at leisure I'll discourse with him   95
　　In our own language.

FLAMINEO.   I beseech you do, –

　　Exit ZANCHE.

　　How is 't brave soldier? O that I had seen
　　Some of your iron days! I pray relate
　　Some of your service to us.

FRANCISCO. 'Tis a ridiculous thing for a man to be his   100
　　own chronicle, – I did never wash my mouth with mine
　　own praise for fear of getting a stinking breath.

MARCELLO. You're too stoical. The duke will expect other
　　discourse from you –

FRANCISCO. I shall never flatter him, – I have studied man   105
　　too much to do that: what difference is between the duke
　　and I? no more than between two bricks; all made of one clay.

Only 't may be one is plac'd on the top of a turret; the other
in the bottom of a well by mere chance; if I were plac'd as
high as the duke, I should stick as fast; make as fair a show;   110
and bear out weather equally.

FLAMINEO. If this soldier had a patent to beg in churches,
then he would tell them stories.

MARCELLO. I have been a soldier too.

FRANCISCO. How have you thriv'd?   115

MARCELLO. Faith poorly.

FRANCISCO. That's the misery of peace. Only outsides are
then respected: as ships seem very great upon the river,
which show very little upon the seas: so some men i' th'
court seem Colossuses in a chamber, who if they came   120
into the field would appear pitiful pigmies.

FLAMINEO. Give me a fair room yet hung with arras, and
some great cardinal to lug me by th' ears as his endeared
minion.   124

FRANCISCO. And thou may'st do the devil knows what villainy.

FLAMINEO. And safely.

FRANCISCO. Right; you shall see in the country in harvest
time, pigeons, though they destroy never so much corn, the
farmer dare not present the fowling-piece to them! why?
because they belong to the lord of the manor; whilst your   130
poor sparrows that belong to the Lord of heaven, they go
to the pot for 't.

FLAMINEO. I will now give you some politic instruction.
The duke says he will give you pension; that's but bare
promise: get it under his hand. For I have known men that   135
have come from serving against the Turk; for three or four
months they have had pension to buy them new wooden
legs and fresh plasters; but after 'twas not to be had. And
this miserable courtesy shows, as if a tormenter should give
hot cordial drinks to one three-quarters dead o' th' rack,   140
only to fetch the miserable soul again to endure more
dog-days.

Enter HORTENSIO, *a* YOUNG LORD, ZANCHE, *and two more.*

How now, gallants; what are they ready for the barriers?

[*Exit* FRANCISCO.]

YOUNG LORD. Yes: the lords are putting on their armour.

HORTENSIO. What's he?   145

FLAMINEO. A new up-start: one that swears like a falc'ner,
and will lie in the duke's ear day by day like a maker of
almanacs; and yet I knew him since he came to th' court
smell worse of sweat than an under-tennis-court
keeper.   150

HORTENSIO. Look you, yonder's your sweet mistress.

FLAMINEO. Thou art my sworn brother, I'll tell thee, –
I do love that Moor, that witch, very constrainedly: she
knows some of my villainy; I do love her, just as a man holds
a wolf by the ears. But for fear of turning upon me, and   155
pulling out my throat, I would let her go to the devil.

HORTENSIO. I hear she claims marriage of thee.

FLAMINEO. 'Faith, I made to her some such dark promise,
and in seeking to fly from 't I run on, like a frighted dog with
a bottle at 's tail, that fain would bite it off and yet dares not   160
look behind him. – Now my precious gipsy!

ZANCHE. Ay, your love to me rather cools than heats.

FLAMINEO. Marry, I am the sounder lover, – we have many
wenches about the town heat too fast.   164

HORTENSIO. What do you think of these perfum'd gallants then?

FLAMINEO. Their satin cannot save them. I am confident
They have a certain spice of the disease,
For they that sleep with dogs, shall rise with fleas.

ZANCHE. Believe it! A little painting and gay clothes make
you loathe me.   170

FLAMINEO. How? love a lady for painting or gay apparel?
I'll unkennel one example more for thee. Æsop had a foolish

dog that let go the flesh to catch the shadow. I would have
courtiers be better diners.

ZANCHE. You remember your oaths.   175

FLAMINEO. Lovers' oaths are like mariners' prayers, uttered
in extremity; but when the tempest is o'er, and that the
vessel leaves tumbling, they fall from protesting to
drinking. And yet amongst gentlemen protesting and
drinking go together, and agree as well as shoemakers   180
and Westphalia bacon. They are both drawers on; for
drink draws on protestation; and protestation draws on
more drink. Is not this discourse better now than the
morality of your sunburnt gentleman?

Enter CORNELIA.

CORNELIA. Is this your perch, you haggard? fly to th' stews.   185

[*Strikes* ZANCHE.]

FLAMINEO. You should be clapp'd by th' heels now: strike i' th'
court!

[*Exit* CORNELIA.]

ZANCHE. She's good for nothing but to make her maids
Catch cold a' nights; they dare not use a bed-staff,
For fear of her light fingers.

MARCELLO.   You're a strumpet.
An impudent one.

[*Kicks* ZANCHE.]

FLAMINEO.   Why do you kick her? say,   190
Do you think that she's like a walnut tree?
Must she be cudgell'd ere she bear good fruit?

MARCELLO. She brags that you shall marry her.

FLAMINEO.   What then?

MARCELLO. I had rather she were pitch'd upon a stake
In some new-seeded garden, to affright   195
Her fellow crows thence.

FLAMINEO.   You're a boy, a fool, –
  Be guardian to your hound, I am of age.

MARCELLO. If I take her near you I'll cut her throat.

FLAMINEO. With a fan of feathers?

MARCELLO.   And for you, – I'll whip
  This folly from you.

FLAMINEO.   Are you choleric?   200
  I'll purge 't with rhubarb.

HORTENSIO.   O your brother!

FLAMINEO.   Hang him.
  He wrongs me most that ought t' offend me least, –
  I do suspect my mother play'd foul play
  When she conceiv'd thee.

MARCELLO.   Now by all my hopes,
  Like the two slaught'red sons of Œdipus,   205
  The very flames of our affection
  Shall turn two ways. Those words I'll make thee answer
  With thy heart blood.

FLAMINEO.   Do – like the geese in the progress,
  You know where you shall find me, – [*Exit.*]

MARCELLO.   Very good, –
  And thou beest a noble friend, bear him my sword,   210
  And bid him fit the length on 't.

YOUNG LORD.   Sir I shall.

  [*Exeunt all but* ZANCHE.] *Enter* FRANCISCO *the Duke of Florence*
  [*disguised as Mulinassar*].

ZANCHE [*aside*]. He comes. Hence petty thought of my disgrace, –
  [*To him.*] I ne'er lov'd my complexion till now,
  Cause I may boldly say without a blush,
  I love you.

FRANCISCO. Your love is untimely sown, –   215
  There's a spring at Michaelmas, but 'tis but a faint one, –
  I am sunk in years, and I have vowed never to marry.

ZANCHE. Alas! poor maids get more lovers than husbands, –
yet you mistake my wealth. For, as when ambassadors
are sent to congratulate princes, there's commonly sent   220
along with them a rich present; so that though the prince
like not the ambassador's person nor words, yet he likes
well of the presentment; so I may come to you in the
same manner, and be better loved for my dowry than
my virtue.   225

FRANCISCO. I'll think on the motion.

ZANCHE. Do, – I'll now detain you no longer. At your better
leisure I'll tell you things shall startle your blood.

Nor blame me that this passion I reveal;
Lovers die inward that their flames conceal.   230

FRANCISCO [*aside*]. Of all intelligence this may prove the best, –
Sure I shall draw strange fowl, from this foul nest.

Exeunt.

Act Five, Scene Two

Enter MARCELLO *and* CORNELIA.

CORNELIA. I hear a whispering all about the court,
You are to fight, – who is your opposite?
What is the quarrel?

MARCELLO.   'Tis an idle rumour.

CORNELIA. Will you dissemble? sure you do not well
To fright me thus, – you never look thus pale   5
But when you are most angry. I do charge you
Upon my blessing; – nay I'll call the duke,
And he shall school you.

MARCELLO.   Publish not a fear
Which would convert to laughter; 'tis not so, –
Was not this crucifix my father's?

CORNELIA.   Yes.   10

MARCELLO. I have heard you say, giving my brother suck,
　　He took the crucifix between his hands,

　　Enter FLAMINEO.

　　And broke a limb off.

CORNELIA.　　　　　　　Yes: but 'tis mended.

FLAMINEO. I have brought your weapon back.

　　FLAMINEO *runs* MARCELLO *through.*

CORNELIA.　　　　　　　　　　Ha, O my horror!

MARCELLO. You have brought it home indeed.

CORNELIA.　　　　　　　　　Help, – O he's murdered.

FLAMINEO. Do you turn your gall up? I'll to sanctuary,　　16
　　And send a surgeon to you.

　　[*Exit.*] *Enter* CARLO, HORTENSIO, PEDRO.

HORTENSIO.　　　　　　How? o' th' ground?

MARCELLO. O mother now remember what I told
　　Of breaking off the crucifix: – farewell –
　　There are some sins which heaven doth duly punish　　20
　　In a whole family. This it is to rise
　　By all dishonest means. Let all men know
　　That tree shall long time keep a steady foot
　　Whose branches spread no wider than the root. [*Dies.*]

CORNELIA. O my perpetual sorrow!

HORTENSIO.　　　　　　　　Virtuous Marcello.　　25
　　He's dead: pray leave him lady; come, you shall.

CORNELIA. Alas he is not dead: he's in a trance.

　　Why here's nobody shall get any thing by his death. Let
　　me call him again for God's sake.

CARLO. I would you were deceiv'd.　　30

CORNELIA. O you abuse me, you abuse me, you abuse me.
　　How many have gone away thus for lack of tendance;
　　rear up's head, rear up's head; his bleeding inward will
　　kill him.

HORTENSIO. You see he is departed.   35

CORNELIA. Let me come to him; give me him as he is, if he
be turn'd to earth; let me but give him one hearty kiss, and
you shall put us both into one coffin: fetch a looking-glass,
see if his breath will not stain it; or pull out some feathers
from my pillow, and lay them to his lips, – will you lose him   40
for a little pains-taking?

HORTENSIO. Your kindest office is to pray for him.

CORNELIA. Alas! I would not pray for him yet. He may live to lay
me i' th' ground, and pray for me, if you'll let me come to him.

Enter BRACCIANO *all armed, save the beaver, with* FLAMINEO,
[FRANCISCO *disguised as Mulinassar, a Page, and* LODOVICO
disguised].

BRACCIANO. Was this your handiwork?   45

FLAMINEO. It was my misfortune.

CORNELIA. He lies, he lies, – he did not kill him: these have
kill'd him, that would not let him be better look'd to.

BRACCIANO. Have comfort my griev'd mother.

CORNELIA. O you screech-owl!   50

HORTENSIO. Forbear, good madam.

CORNELIA. Let me go, let me go.

She rams to FLAMINEO *with her knife drawn and coming to him
lets it fall.*

The God of heaven forgive thee. Dost not wonder
I pray for thee? I'll tell thee what's the reason, –
I have scarce breath to number twenty minutes;   55
I'd not spend that in cursing. Fare thee well –
Half of thyself lies there: and may'st thou live
To fill an hour-glass with his mould'red ashes,
To tell how thou shouldst spend the time to come
In blest repentance.

BRACCIANO.   Mother, pray tell me   60
How came he by his death? what was the quarrel?

CORNELIA. Indeed my younger boy presum'd too much
    Upon his manhood, gave him bitter words;
    Drew his sword first; and so I know not how,
    For I was out of my wits, he fell with's head   65
    Just in my bosom.

PAGE. This is not time madam.

CORNELIA.   I pray thee peace.
    One arrow's graz'd already; it were vain
    T' lose this: for that will ne'er be found again.

BRACCIANO. Go, bear the body to Cornelia's lodging: 70
    And we command that none acquaint our duchess
    With this sad accident: for you Flamineo,
    Hark you, I will not grant your pardon.

FLAMINEO.   No?

BRACCIANO. Only a lease of your life. And that shall last
    But for one day. Thou shalt be forc'd each evening   75
    To renew it, or be hang'd.

FLAMINEO.   At your pleasure.

    LODOVICO *sprinkles* BRACCIANO's *beaver with a poison.*

Your will is law now, I'll not meddle with it.

BRACCIANO. You once did brave me in your sister's lodging;
    I'll now keep you in awe for 't. Where's our beaver?

FRANCISCO [*aside*]. He calls for his destruction. Noble youth,   80
    I pity thy sad fate. Now to the barriers.
    This shall his passage to the black lake further, –
    The last good deed he did, he pardon'd murther.

    Exeunt.

Act Five, Scene Three

Charges and shouts. They fight at barriers; first single pairs, then three to three.
Enter BRACCIANO *and* FLAMINEO *with others* [*following, including*
VITTORIA, GIOVANNI, *and* FRANCISCO *disguised as Mulinassar*].

BRACCIANO. An armourer! Ud's death an armourer!

FLAMINEO. Armourer; where's the armourer?

BRACCIANO. Tear off my beaver.

FLAMINEO.   Are you hurt, my lord?

BRACCIANO. O my brain's on fire,

        Enter ARMOURER.

                                    the helmet is poison'd.   4

ARMOURER. My lord upon my soul –

BRACCIANO.   Away with him to torture.

        [*Exit* ARMOURER, *guarded.*]

    There are some great ones that have hand in this,
    And near about me.

VITTORIA.   O my loved lord, – poisoned?

FLAMINEO. Remove the bar: here's unfortunate revels, –
    Call the physicians;

        Enter two PHYSICIANS.

                          a plague upon you;
    We have too much of your cunning here already.   10
    I fear the ambassadors are likewise poison'd.

BRACCIANO. O I am gone already: the infection
    Flies to the brain and heart. O thou strong heart!
    There's such a covenant 'tween the world and it,
    They're loth to break.

GIOVANNI.   O my most loved father!   15

BRACCIANO. Remove the boy away, –
    Where's this good woman? had I infinite worlds
    They were too little for thee. Must I leave thee?

What say yon screech-owls, is the venom mortal?

PHYSICIANS. Most deadly.

BRACCIANO.   Most corrupted politic hangman!   20
   You kill without book; but your art to save
   Fails you as oft as great men's needy friends.
   I that have given life to offending slaves
   And wretched murderers, have I not power
   To lengthen mine own a twelve-month?   25
   [*To* VITTORIA.] Do not kiss me, for I shall poison thee.
   This unction is sent from the great Duke of Florence.

FRANCISCO. Sir be of comfort.

BRACCIANO. O thou soft natural death, that art joint-twin
   To sweetest slumber: no rough-bearded comet   30
   Stares on thy mild departure: the dull owl
   Beats not against thy casement: the hoarse wolf
   Scents not thy carrion. Pity winds thy corse,
   Whilst horror waits on princes.

VITTORIA. I am lost for ever.   35

BRACCIANO. How miserable a thing it is to die
   'Mongst women howling!

   [*Enter* LODOVICO *and* GASPARO, *in the habit of Capuchins.*]

                What are those?

FLAMINEO.   Franciscans.
   They have brought the extreme unction.

BRACCIANO. On pain of death, let no man name death to me,
   It is a word infinitely terrible, –   40
   Withdraw into our cabinet.

   Exeunt but FRANCISCO *and* FLAMINEO.

FLAMINEO. To see what solitariness is about dying princes.
   As heretofore they have unpeopled towns; divorc'd friends,
   and made great houses unhospitable: so now, O justice!
   where are their flatterers now? Flatterers are but the   45
   shadows of princes' bodies – the least thick cloud makes
   them invisible.

FRANCISCO. There's great moan made for him.

FLAMINEO. 'Faith, for some few hours salt water will run most
 plentifully in every office o' th' court. But believe it: most 50
 of them do but weep over their stepmothers' graves.

FRANCISCO. How mean you?

FLAMINEO. Why? They dissemble, as some men do that live
 within compass o' th' verge.

FRANCISCO. Come you have thriv'd well under him. 55

FLAMINEO. 'Faith, like a wolf in a woman's breast; I have been
 fed with poultry; but for money, understand me, I had as
 good a will to cozen him, as e'er an officer of them all. But
 I had not cunning enough to do it.

FRANCISCO. What did'st thou think of him? 'faith speak freely. 60

FLAMINEO. He was a kind of statesman, that would sooner
 have reckon'd how many cannon-bullets he had discharged
 against a town, to count his expense that way, than how
 many of his valiant and deserving subjects he lost before it.

FRANCISCO. O, speak well of the duke. 65

FLAMINEO. I have done. Wilt hear some of my court wisdom?

Enter LODOVICO [*disguised as before*].

To reprehend princes is dangerous: and to over commend
some of them is palpable lying.

FRANCISCO. How is it with the duke?

LODOVICO.   Most deadly ill.
He's fall'n into a strange distraction. 70
He talks of battles and monopolies,
Levying of taxes, and from that descends
To the most brain-sick language. His mind fastens
On twenty several objects, which confound
Deep sense with folly. Such a fearful end 75
May teach some men that bear too lofty crest,
Though they live happiest, yet they die not best.
He hath conferr'd the whole state of the dukedom

Upon your sister, till the prince arrive
At mature age.

FLAMINEO.   There's some good luck in that yet.   80

FRANCISCO. See here he comes.

Enter BRACCIANO, *presented in a bed,* VITTORIA *and others,*
[*including* GASPARO, *disguised as before*].

                              There's death in 's face already.

VITTORIA. O my good lord!

BRACCIANO.   Away, you have abus'd me.

*These speeches are several kinds of distractions and in the action
should appear so.*

You have convey'd coin forth our territories;
Bought and sold offices; oppress'd the poor,
And I ne'er dreamt on 't. Make up your accounts;   85
I'll now be mine own steward.

FLAMINEO.   Sir, have patience.

BRACCIANO. Indeed I am too blame.
    For did you ever hear the dusky raven
    Chide blackness? or was 't ever known the devil
    Rail'd against cloven creatures?

VITTORIA.   O my lord!   90

BRACCIANO. Let me have some quails to supper.

FLAMINEO.   Sir, you shall.

BRACCIANO. No: some fried dog-fish. Your quails feed on poison, –
    That old dog-fox, that politician Florence, –
    I'll forswear hunting and turn dog-killer;
    Rare! I'll be friends with him: for mark you, sir, one dog   95
    Still sets another a-barking: peace, peace,
    Yonder's a fine slave come in now.

FLAMINEO.   Where?

BRACCIANO.   Why there.
    In a blue bonnet, and a pair of breeches

With a great codpiece. Ha, ha, ha,
Look you his codpiece is stuck full of pins   100
With pearls o' th' head of them. Do not you know him?

FLAMINEO. No, my lord.

BRACCIANO.   Why 'tis the devil.
I know him by a great rose he wears on 's shoe
To hide his cloven foot. I'll dispute with him.
He's a rare linguist.

VITTORIA.   My lord here's nothing.   105

BRACCIANO. Nothing? rare! nothing! when I want money,
Our treasury is empty; there is nothing, –
I'll not be us'd thus.

VITTORIA.   O! lie still, my lord –

BRACCIANO. See, see, Flamineo that kill'd his brother
Is dancing on the ropes there: and he carries   110
A money-bag in each hand, to keep him even,
For fear of breaking's neck. And there's a lawyer
In a gown whipt with velvet, stares and gapes
When the money will fall. How the rogue cuts capers!
It should have been in a halter.   115
'Tis there; what's she?

FLAMINEO.   Vittoria, my lord.

BRACCIANO. Ha, ha, ha. Her hair is sprinkled with arras
powder, that makes her look as if she had sinn'd in the
pastry. What's he?

FLAMINEO. A divine my lord.   120

BRACCIANO. He will be drunk: avoid him: th' argument is
fearful when churchmen stagger in 't.

Look you; six gray rats that have lost their tails,
Crawl up the pillow, – send for a rat-catcher.
I'll do a miracle: I'll free the court   125
From all foul vermin. Where's Flamineo?

FLAMINEO. I do not like that he names me so often,
Especially on 's death-bed: 'tis a sign

I shall not live long: see he's near his end.

BRACCIANO *seems here near his end.* LODOVICO *and*
GASPARO *in the habit of Capuchins present him in his bed*
with a crucifix and hallowed candle.

LODOVICO. Pray give us leave: *Attende Domine Bracciane,* –   130

FLAMINEO. See, see, how firmly he doth fix his eye
Upon the crucifix.

VITTORIA.   O hold it constant.
It settles his wild spirits; and so his eyes
Melt into tears.

LODOVICO (*by the crucifix*). *Domine Bracciane, solebas in*   135
bello tutus esse tuo clypeo, nùnc hunc clypeum hosti tuo opponas
infernali.

GASPARO (*by the hallowed taper*). *Olim hastâ valuisti in bello;*
nùnc hanc sacram hastam vibrabis contra hostem animarum.

LODOVICO. *Attende Domine Bracciane si nunc quòque probas*   140
ea quæ acta sunt inter nos, flecte caput in dextrum.

GASPARO. *Esto securus Domine Bracciane: cogita quantum*
habeas meritorum – denique memineris meam animam pro tua
oppignoratam si quid esset periculi.

LODOVICO. *Si nùnc quoque probas ea quæ acta sunt inter nos,*   145
flecte caput in lævum.

He is departing: pray stand all apart,
And let us only whisper in his ears
Some private meditations, which our order
Permits you not to hear.

Here the rest being departed LODOVICO *and* GASPARO
discover themselves.

GASPARO.   Bracciano.   150

LODOVICO. Devil Bracciano. Thou art damn'd.

GASPARO.   Perpetually.

LODOVICO. A slave condemn'd, and given up to the gallows

Is thy great lord and master.

GASPARO.   True: for thou
   Art given up to the devil.

LODOVICO.   O you slave!
   You that were held the famous politician;   155
   Whose art was poison.

GASPARO.   And whose conscience murder.

LODOVICO. That would have broke your wife's neck down the stairs
   Ere she was poison'd.

GASPARO.   That had your villainous sallets –

LODOVICO. And fine embroidered bottles, and perfumes
   Equally mortal with a winter plague –   160

GASPARO. Now there's mercury –

LODOVICO.   And copperas –

GASPARO.   And quicksilver –

LODOVICO. With other devilish pothecary stuff
   A-melting in your politic brains: dost hear?

GASPARO. This is Count Lodovico.

LODOVICO.   This Gasparo.
   And thou shalt die like a poor rogue.

GASPARO.   And stink   165
   Like a dead fly-blown dog.

LODOVICO.   And be forgotten
   Before thy funeral sermon.

BRACCIANO.   Vittoria?
   Vittoria!

LODOVICO. O the cursed devil,
   Come to himself again! We are undone.

Enter VITTORIA *and the* ATTENDANTS.

GASPARO [*aside*]. Strangle him in private.   170
   [*Aloud.*] What? will you call him again

To live in treble torments? for charity,
For Christian charity, avoid the chamber.

[*Exeunt* VITTORIA *etc.*]

LODOVICO. You would prate, sir. This is a true-love knot
    Sent from the Duke of Florence.

BRACCIANO *is strangled.*

GASPARO.   What – is it done?   175

LODOVICO. The snuff is out. No woman-keeper i' th' world,
    Though she had practis'd seven year at the pest-house,
    Could have done 't quaintlier. My lords he's dead.

[*Re-enter* VITTORIA, FRANCISCO, *and* FLAMINEO, *with*
ATTENDANTS.]

OMNES. Rest to his soul.

VITTORIA.   O me! this place is hell.

Exit VITTORIA[, *followed by all except* LODOVICO,
FRANCISCO, *and* FLAMINEO].

FRANCISCO. How heavily she takes it.

FLAMINEO.   O yes, yes;   180
    Had women navigable rivers in their eyes
    They would dispend them all; surely I wonder
    Why we should wish more rivers to the city,
    When they sell water so good cheap. I'll tell thee,
    These are but moonish shades of griefs or fears,   185
    There's nothing sooner dry than women's tears.
    Why here's an end of all my harvest, he has given me nothing –
    Court promises! Let wise men count them curst
    For while you live he that scores best pays worst.

FRANCISCO. Sure, this was Florence' doing.

FLAMINEO.   Very likely.   190
    Those are found weighty strokes which come from th' hand,
    But those are killing strokes which come from th' head.
    O the rare tricks of a Machivillian!

He doth not come like a gross plodding slave
And buffet you to death: no, my quaint knave,   195
He tickles you to death; makes you die laughing;
As if you had swallow'd down a pound of saffron –
You see the feat, – 'tis practis'd in a trice
To teach court-honesty it jumps on ice.

FRANCISCO. Now have the people liberty to talk   200
    And descant on his vices.

FLAMINEO.   Misery of princes,
    That must of force be censur'd by their slaves!
    Not only blam'd for doing things are ill,
    But for not doing all that all men will.
    One were better be a thresher.   205
    Ud's death, I would fain speak with this duke yet.

FRANCISCO. Now he's dead?

FLAMINEO. I cannot conjure; but if prayers or oaths
    Will get to th' speech of him, though forty devils
    Wait on him in his livery of flames,   210
    I'll speak to him, and shake him by the hand,
    Though I be blasted.

    Exit FLAMINEO.

FRANCISCO.   Excellent Lodovico!
    What? did you terrify him at the last gasp?

LODOVICO. Yes; and so idly, that the duke had like
    T' have terrified us.

FRANCISCO.   How?

    Enter [ZANCHE] *the Moor.*

LODOVICO.   You shall hear that hereafter, –   215
    [*Aside.*] See! yon's the infernal, that would make up sport.
    Now to the revelation of that secret
    She promis'd when she fell in love with you.

FRANCISCO. You're passionately met in this sad world.

ZANCHE. I would have you look up, sir; these court tears   220

Claim not your tribute to them. Let those weep
That guiltily partake in the sad cause.
I knew last night by a sad dream I had
Some mischief would ensue; yet to say truth
My dream most concern'd you.

LODOVICO.   Shall's fall a-dreaming?   225

FRANCISCO. Yes, and for fashion sake I'll dream with her.

ZANCHE. Methought sir, you came stealing to my bed.

FRANCISCO. Wilt thou believe me sweeting? by this light
    I was a-dreamt on thee too: for methought
    I saw thee naked.

ZANCHE.   Fie sir! as I told you,   230
    Methought you lay down by me.

FRANCISCO.   So dreamt I;
    And lest thou shouldst take cold, I cover'd thee
    With this Irish mantle.

ZANCHE.   Verily, I did dream
    You were somewhat bold with me; but to come to 't.

LODOVICO. How? how? I hope you will not go to 't here.   235

FRANCISCO. Nay: you must hear my dream out.

ZANCHE.   Well, sir, forth.

FRANCISCO. When I threw the mantle o'er thee, thou didst laugh
    Exceedingly methought.

ZANCHE.   Laugh?

FRANCISCO.   And cried'st out,
    The hair did tickle thee.

ZANCHE.   There was a dream indeed.

LODOVICO. Mark her I prithee, – she simpers like the suds   240
    A collier hath been wash'd in.

ZANCHE. Come, sir; good fortune tends you; I did tell you
    I would reveal a secret, – Isabella
    The Duke of Florence' sister was empoison'd,

By a 'fum'd picture: and Camillo's neck   245
Was broke by damn'd Flamineo; the mischance
Laid on a vaulting-horse.

FRANCISCO.   Most strange!

ZANCHE.   Most true.

LODOVICO. The bed of snakes is broke.

ZANCHE. I sadly do confess I had a hand
In the black deed.

FRANCISCO.   Thou kept'st their counsel, –

ZANCHE.   Right, –   250
For which, urg'd with contrition, I intend
This night to rob Vittoria.

LODOVICO.   Excellent penitence!
Usurers dream on 't while they sleep out sermons.

ZANCHE. To further our escape, I have entreated
Leave to retire me, till the funeral,   255
Unto a friend i' th' country. That excuse
Will further our escape. In coin and jewels
I shall, at least, make good unto your use
An hundred thousand crowns.

FRANCISCO.   O noble wench!

LODOVICO. Those crowns we'll share.

ZANCHE.   It is a dowry,   260
Methinks, should make that sunburnt proverb false,
And wash the Ethiop white.

FRANCISCO.   It shall, – away!

ZANCHE. Be ready for our flight.

FRANCISCO.   An hour 'fore day.

Exit [ZANCHE] *the Moor.*

O strange discovery! why till now we knew not
The circumstance of either of their deaths.   265

[Re-]enter [ZANCHE the] Moor.

ZANCHE. You'll wait about midnight in the chapel.

FRANCISCO.   There.

[Exit ZANCHE.]

LODOVICO. Why now our action's justified, –

FRANCISCO.   Tush for justice.
    What harms it justice? we now, like the partridge
    Purge the disease with laurel: for the fame
    Shall crown the enterprize and quit the shame.   270

    Exeunt.

Act Five, Scene Four

Enter FLAMINEO *and* GASPARO *at one door, another way*
GIOVANNI *attended.*

GASPARO. The young duke: did you e'er see a sweeter prince?

FLAMINEO. I have known a poor woman's bastard better
    favour'd, – this is behind him: now, to his face all com-
    parisons were hateful: wise was the courtly peacock, that
    being a great minion, and being compar'd for beauty,   5
    by some dottrels that stood by, to the kingly eagle, said
    the eagle was a far fairer bird than herself, not in respect
    of her feathers, but in respect of her long tallants. His will
    grow out in time, –

    My gracious lord.   10

GIOVANNI. I pray leave me sir.

FLAMINEO. Your grace must be merry: 'tis I have cause to
    mourn, for wot you what said the little boy that rode behind
    his father on horseback?

GIOVANNI. Why, what said he?   15

FLAMINEO. 'When you are dead father' (said he) 'I hope

then I shall ride in the saddle', – O 'tis a brave thing for a
man to sit by himself: he may stretch himself in the stirrups,
look about, and see the whole compass of the hemisphere, –
you're now, my lord, i' th' saddle.   20

GIOVANNI. Study your prayers, sir, and be penitent, –
'Twere fit you'd think on what hath former bin, –
I have heard grief nam'd the eldest child of sin.

Exit GIOVANNI [*and all except* FLAMINEO].

FLAMINEO. Study my prayers? he threatens me divinely, –
I am falling to pieces already, – I care not, though, like   25
Anacharsis, I were pounded to death in a mortar. And
yet that death were fitter for usurers' gold and themselves to be beaten together, to make a most cordial
cullis for the devil.

He hath his uncle's villainous look already,   30

Enter COURTIER.

In *decimo-sexto*. Now sir, what are you?

COURTIER. It is the pleasure sir, of the young duke
That you forbear the presence, and all rooms
That owe him reverence.

FLAMINEO. So, the wolf and the raven   35
Are very pretty fools when they are young.
Is it your office, sir, to keep me out?

COURTIER. So the duke wills.

FLAMINEO. Verily, master courtier, extremity is not to be
used in all offices: say that a gentlewoman were taken out   40
of her bed about midnight, and committed to Castle Angelo,
to the tower yonder, with nothing about her, but her smock:
would it not show a cruel part in the gentleman porter to
lay claim to her upper garment, pull it o'er her head and
ears; and put her in nak'd?   45

COURTIER. Very good: you are merry. [*Exit.*]

FLAMINEO. Doth he make a court ejectment of me? A flaming
firebrand casts more smoke without a chimney, than within 't.

I'll smoor some of them.

Enter [FRANCISCO *Duke of*] *Florence,* [*disguised as Mulinassar*].

How now? Thou art sad.   50

FRANCISCO. I met even now with the most piteous sight.

FLAMINEO. Thou met'st another here – a pitiful
  Degraded courtier.

FRANCISCO.   Your reverend mother
  Is grown a very old woman in two hours.
  I found them winding of Marcello's corse;   55
  And there is such a solemn melody
  'Tween doleful songs, tears, and sad elegies: –
  Such, as old grandames, watching by the dead,
  Were wont t' outwear the nights with; – that believe me
  I had no eyes to guide me forth the room,   60
  They were so o'ercharg'd with water.

FLAMINEO.   I will see them.

FRANCISCO. 'Twere much uncharity in you: for your sight
  Will add unto their tears.

FLAMINEO.   I will see them.
  They are behind the traverse. I'll discover
  Their superstitious howling.   65

  [*Draws the traverse curtain.*] CORNELIA, [ZANCHE] *the Moor and*
  three other LADIES *discovered, winding* MARCELLO's *corse.*

  A song.

CORNELIA. This rosemary is wither'd, pray get fresh;
  I would have these herbs grow up in his grave
  When I am dead and rotten. Reach the bays,
  I'll tie a garland here about his head:
  'Twill keep my boy from lightning. This sheet   70
  I have kept this twenty year, and every day
  Hallow'd it with my prayers, – I did not think
  He should have wore it.

ZANCHE.   Look you; who are yonder?

CORNELIA. O reach me the flowers.

ZANCHE. Her ladyship's foolish.

LADY.   Alas! her grief   75
  Hath turn'd her child again.

CORNELIA.   You're very welcome.
  There's rosemary for you, and rue for you, (*To* FLAMINEO.)
  Heart's-ease for you. I pray make much of it.
  I have left more for myself.

FRANCISCO.   Lady, who's this?

CORNELIA. You are, I take it, the grave-maker.   80

FLAMINEO.   So.

ZANCHE. 'Tis Flamineo.

CORNELIA. Will you make me such a fool? here's a white hand:

  CORNELIA *doth this in several forms of distraction.*

  Can blood so soon be wash'd out? Let me see, –
  When screech-owls croak upon the chimney-tops,
  And the strange cricket i' th' oven sings and hops,   85
  When yellow spots do on your hands appear,
  Be certain then you of a corse shall hear.
  Out upon 't, how 'tis speckled! h' as handled a toad sure.

  Cowslip-water is good for the memory: pray buy me three
  ounces of 't.   90

FLAMINEO. I would I were from hence.

CORNELIA.   Do you hear, sir?
  I'll give you a saying which my grandmother
  Was wont, when she heard the bell toll, to sing o'er
  Unto her lute.

FLAMINEO.   Do and you will, do.

CORNELIA. *Call for the robin-red-breast and the wren,*   95
  Since o'er shady groves they hover,
  And with leaves and flow'rs do cover
  The friendless bodies of unburied men.

Call unto his funeral dole
The ant, the field-mouse, and the mole   100
To rear him hillocks, that shall keep him warm,
And (when gay tombs are robb'd) sustain no harm, –
But keep the wolf far thence, that's foe to men,
For with his nails he'll dig them up agen.
They would not bury him 'cause he died in a quarrel   105
But I have an answer for them.
Let holy church receive him duly
Since he paid the church tithes truly.
His wealth is summ'd, and this is all his store:
This poor men get; and great men get no more.   110
Now the wares are gone, we may shut up shop.
Bless you all good people, –

Exeunt CORNELIA, [ZANCHE,] *and* LADIES.

FLAMINEO. I have a strange thing in me, to th' which
I cannot give a name, without it be
Compassion, – I pray leave me.   115

Exit FRANCISCO.

This night I'll know the utmost of my fate,
I'll be resolv'd what my rich sister means
T' assign me for my service: I have liv'd
Riotously ill, like some that live in court;
And sometimes, when my face was full of smiles   120
Have felt the maze of conscience in my breast.
Oft gay and honour'd robes those tortures try, –
We think cag'd birds sing, when indeed they cry.

Enter BRACCIANO'*s Ghost, in his leather cassock and breeches, boots,*
[*and*] *a cowl,* [*in his hand*] *a pot of lily-flowers with a skull in 't.*

Ha! I can stand thee. Nearer, nearer yet.
What a mockery hath death made of thee?   125
Thou look'st sad.
In what place art thou? in yon starry gallery,
Or in the cursed dungeon? No? not speak?
Pray, sir, resolve me, what religion's best
For a man to die in? or is it in your knowledge   130

To answer me how long I have to live?
That's the most necessary question.
Not answer? Are you still like some great men
That only walk like shadows up and down,
And to no purpose? say: –

The GHOST *throws earth upon him and shows him the skull.*

What's that? O fatal! he throws earth upon me.   136
A dead man's skull beneath the roots of flowers.
I pray speak sir, – our Italian churchmen
Make us believe dead men hold conference
With their familiars, and many times   140
Will come to bed to them, and eat with them.

Exit GHOST.

He's gone; and see, the skull and earth are vanish'd.
This is beyond melancholy.
I do dare my fate
To do its worst. Now to my sister's lodging,   145
And sum up all these horrors; the disgrace
The prince threw on me; next the piteous sight
Of my dead brother; and my mother's dotage;
And last this terrible vision. All these
Shall with Vittoria's bounty turn to good,   150
Or I will drown this weapon in her blood.

Exit.

Act Five, Scene Five

Enter FRANCISCO, LODOVICO, *and* HORTENSIO
[*overhearing them*].

LODOVICO. My lord upon my soul you shall no further:
    You have most ridiculously engag'd yourself
    Too far already. For my part, I have paid
    All my debts, so if I should chance to fall
    My creditors fall not with me; and I vow   5

To quite all in this bold assembly
To the meanest follower. My lord leave the city,
Or I'll forswear the murder.

FRANCISCO.   Farewell Lodovico.
If thou dost perish in this glorious act,
I'll rear unto thy memory that fame   10
Shall in the ashes keep alive thy name.

[*Exeunt* FRANCISCO *and* LODOVICO *severally.*]

HORTENSIO. There's some black deed on foot. I'll presently
Down to the citadel, and raise some force.
These strong court factions that do brook no checks,
In the career oft break the riders' necks.   15

[*Exit.*]

Act Five, Scene Six

Enter VITTORIA *with a book in her hand;* ZANCHE, [*and*]
FLAMINEO, *following them.*

FLAMINEO. What are you at your prayers? Give o'er.

VITTORIA.   How ruffin?

FLAMINEO. I come to you 'bout worldly business:
Sit down, sit down: – nay stay blowze, you may hear it, –
The doors are fast enough.

VITTORIA.   Ha, are you drunk?

FLAMINEO. Yes, yes, with wormwood water, – you shall taste   5
Some of it presently.

VITTORIA.   What intends the fury?

FLAMINEO. You are my lord's executrix, and I claim
Reward, for my long service.

VITTORIA.   For your service?

FLAMINEO. Come therefore here is pen and ink, set down

What you will give me.   10

She writes.

VITTORIA. There, –

FLAMINEO.   Ha! have you done already? –
'Tis a most short conveyance.

VITTORIA.   I will read it.
   [*Reads.*] '*I give that portion to thee, and no other,*
   Which Cain groan'd under having slain his brother.'

FLAMINEO. A most courtly patent to beg by.   15

VITTORIA. You are a villain.

FLAMINEO. Is 't come to this? they say affrights cure agues:
   Thou hast a devil in thee; I will try
   If I can scare him from thee: – nay sit still:
   My lord hath left me yet two case of jewels   20
   Shall make me scorn your bounty; you shall see them.

   [*Exit.*]

VITTORIA. Sure he's distracted.

ZANCHE.   O he's desperate –
   For your own safety give him gentle language.

   [*Re-*]*enter* [FLAMINEO] *with two case of pistols.*

FLAMINEO. Look, these are better far at a dead lift
   Than all your jewel house.

VITTORIA.   And yet methinks   25
   These stones have no fair lustre, they are ill set.

FLAMINEO. I'll turn the right side towards you: you shall see
   How they will sparkle.

VITTORIA.   Turn this horror from me:
   What do you want? what would you have me do?
   Is not all mine, yours? have I any children?   30

FLAMINEO. Pray thee good woman do not trouble me
   With this vain worldly business; say your prayers, –
   I made a vow to my deceased lord,

Neither yourself, nor I should outlive him
The numb'ring of four hours.

VITTORIA.   Did he enjoin it?   35

FLAMINEO. He did, and 'twas a deadly jealousy,
Lest any should enjoy thee after him,
That urg'd him vow me to it: – for my death –
I did propound it voluntarily, knowing
If he could not be safe in his own court   40
Being a great duke, what hope then for us?

VITTORIA. This is your melancholy and despair.

FLAMINEO.   Away, –
Fool thou art to think that politicians
Do use to kill the effects of injuries
And let the cause live: shall we groan in irons,   45
Or be a shameful and a weighty burden
To a public scaffold? This is my resolve –
I would not live at any man's entreaty
Nor die at any's bidding.

VITTORIA.   Will you hear me?

FLAMINEO. My life hath done service to other men,   50
My death shall serve mine own turn; make you ready –

VITTORIA. Do you mean to die indeed?

FLAMINEO.   With as much pleasure
As e'er my father gat me.

VITTORIA [aside]. Are the doors lock'd?

ZANCHE [aside]. Yes madam.   55

VITTORIA. Are you grown an atheist? will you turn your body,
Which is the goodly palace of the soul
To the soul's slaughter house? O the cursed devil
Which doth present us with all other sins
Thrice candied o'er; despair with gall and stibium,   60
Yet we carouse it off; – [Aside to ZANCHE.] cry out for help, –
Makes us forsake that which was made for man,
The world, to sink to that was made for devils,

Eternal darkness.

ZANCHE.   Help, help!

FLAMINEO.   I'll stop your throat
With winter plums, –

VITTORIA.   I prithee yet remember,   65
Millions are now in graves, which at last day
Like mandrakes shall rise shrieking.

FLAMINEO.   Leave your prating,
For these are but grammatical laments,
Feminine arguments, and they move me
As some in pulpits move their auditory   70
More with their exclamation than sense
Of reason, or sound doctrine.

ZANCHE [*aside*].   Gentle madam
Seem to consent, only persuade him teach
The way to death; let him die first.

VITTORIA [*aside*]. 'Tis good, I apprehend it, –   75
[*Aloud*.] To kill one's self is meat that we must take
Like pills, not chew't, but quickly swallow it, –
The smart a' th' wound, or weakness of the hand
May else bring treble torments.

FLAMINEO.   I have held it
A wretched and most miserable life,   80
Which is not able to die.

VITTORIA.   O but frailty!
Yet I am now resolv'd, – farewell affliction;
Behold Bracciano, I that while you liv'd
Did make a flaming altar of my heart
To sacrifice unto you; now am ready
To sacrifice heart and all. Farewell Zanche.   85

ZANCHE. How madam! Do you think that I'll outlive you?
Especially when my best self Flamineo
Goes the same voyage.

FLAMINEO.   O most loved Moor!

ZANCHE. Only by all my love let me entreat you; –   90
    Since it is most necessary none of us
    Do violence on ourselves; – let you or I
    Be her sad taster, teach her how to die.

FLAMINEO. Thou dost instruct me nobly, – take these pistols:
    Because my hand is stain'd with blood already,
    Two of these you shall level at my breast,   95
    Th' other 'gainst your own, and so we'll die,
    Most equally contented: but first swear
    Not to outlive me.

VITTORIA *and* ZANCHE. Most religiously.

FLAMINEO. Then here's an end of me: farewell daylight   100
    And O contemptible physic! that dost take
    So long a study, only to preserve
    So short a life, I take my leave of thee.

    Showing the pistols.

    These are two cupping-glasses, that shall draw
    All my infected blood out, – are you ready?

VITTORIA *and* ZANCHE. Ready.

FLAMINEO. Whither shall I go now? O Lucian thy ridicu-
    lous purgatory! to find Alexander the Great cobbling shoes,
    Pompey tagging points, and Julius Caesar making hair
    buttons; Hannibal selling blacking, and Augustus crying   110
    garlic, Charlemagne selling lists by the dozen, and King
    Pippin crying apples in a cart drawn with one horse.

    Whether I resolve to fire, earth, water, air,
    Or all the elements by scruples, I know not
    Nor greatly care, – Shoot, shoot,   115
    Of all deaths the violent death is best,
    For from ourselves it steals ourselves so fast
    The pain once apprehended is quite past.

    They shoot and run to him and tread upon him.

VITTORIA. What – are you dropt?

FLAMINEO. I am mix'd with earth already: as you are noble   120

Perform your vows, and bravely follow me.

VITTORIA. Whither – to hell?

ZANCHE.   To most assured damnation.

VITTORIA. O thou most cursed devil.

ZANCHE.   Thou art caught –

VITTORIA. In thine own engine, – I tread the fire out   125
That would have been my ruin.

FLAMINEO. Will you be perjur'd? what a religious oath was
Styx that the gods never durst swear by and violate? O that
we had such an oath to minister, and to be so well kept
in our courts of justice.

VITTORIA. Think whither thou art going.

ZANCHE.   And remember   130
What villanies thou hast acted.

VITTORIA.   This thy death
Shall make me like a blazing ominous star, –
Look up and tremble.

FLAMINEO.   O I am caught with a springe!

VITTORIA. You see the fox comes many times short home, –
'Tis here prov'd true.

FLAMINEO.   Kill'd with a couple of braches.   135

VITTORIA. No fitter off'ring for the infernal Furies
Than one in whom they reign'd while he was living.

FLAMINEO. O the way's dark and horrid! I cannot see, –
Shall I have no company?

VITTORIA.   O yes thy sins
Do run before thee to fetch fire from hell,   140
To light thee thither.

FLAMINEO.   O I smell soot,
Most stinking soot, the chimney is a-fire, –
My liver's parboil'd like Scotch holy bread;
There's a plumber, laying pipes in my guts, – it scalds;

Wilt thou outlive me?

ZANCHE.   Yes, and drive a stake   145
   Through thy body; for we'll give it out,
   Thou didst this violence upon thyself.

FLAMINEO. O cunning devils! now I have try'd your love,
   And doubled all your reaches. I am not wounded:

FLAMINEO *riseth.*

   The pistols held no bullets: 'twas a plot   150
   To prove your kindness to me; and I live
   To punish your ingratitude, – I knew
   One time or other you would find a way
   To give me a strong potion, – O men
   That lie upon your death-beds, and are haunted   155
   With howling wives, ne'er trust them, – they'll re-marry
   Ere worm pierce your winding-sheet: ere the spider
   Make a thin curtain for your epitaphs.

   How cunning you were to discharge! Do you practise at
   the Artillery Yard? Trust a woman? – never, never;   160
   Bracciano be my precedent: we lay our souls to pawn to
   the devil for a little pleasure, and a woman makes the bill
   of sale. That ever man should marry! For one Hyper-
   mnestra that sav'd her lord and husband, forty-nine of
   her sisters cut their husbands' throats all in one night.   165
   There was a shoal of virtuous horse-leeches.

   Here are two other instruments.

Enter LODOVICO, GASPARO, [*disguised as Capuchins,*] PEDRO,
[*and*] CARLO.

VITTORIA.   Help, help!

FLAMINEO. What noise is that? hah? false keys i' th' court!

LODOVICO. We have brought you a masque.

FLAMINEO.   A matachin it seems,
   By your drawn swords. Churchmen turn'd revellers!   170

CARLO. Isabella, Isabella!

LODOVICO. Do you know us now?

[*They throw off their disguises.*]

FLAMINEO.   Lodovico and Gasparo.

LODOVICO. Yes and that Moor the duke gave pension to
    Was the great Duke of Florence.

VITTORIA.   O we are lost.

FLAMINEO. You shall not take justice from forth my hands, –   175
    O let me kill her. – I'll cut my safety
    Through your coats of steel: Fate's a spaniel,
    We cannot beat it from us: what remains now?
    Let all that do ill, take this precedent:
    Man may his fate foresee, but not prevent.   180
    And of all axioms this shall win the prize:
    'Tis better to be fortunate than wise.

GASPARO. Bind him to the pillar.

VITTORIA.   O your gentle pity! –
    I have seen a blackbird that would sooner fly
    To a man's bosom, than to stay the gripe   185
    Of the fierce sparrow-hawk.

GASPARO.   Your hope deceives you.

VITTORIA. If Florence be i' th' court, would he would kill me.

GASPARO. Fool! Princes give rewards with their own hands,
    But death or punishment by the hands of others.

LODOVICO. Sirrah you once did strike me, – I'll strike you   190
    Into the centre.

FLAMINEO. Thou'lt do it like a hangman; a base hangman;
    Not like a noble fellow, for thou seest
    I cannot strike again.

LODOVICO.   Dost laugh?

FLAMINEO. Wouldst have me die, as I was born, in whining?   195

GASPARO. Recommend yourself to heaven.

FLAMINEO. No I will carry mine own commendations thither.

Please fill in, stamp and return this card if you wish to be kept informed about new publications from Nick Hern Books

Name

Address

Postcode

The most recent NHB catalogue I have is dated

Comments

Nick Hern Books
14 Larden Road
London
W3 7ST
UK

LODOVICO. O could I kill you forty times a day
    And use 't four year together; 'twere too little:
    Nought grieves but that you are too few to feed   200
    The famine of our vengeance. What dost think on?

FLAMINEO. Nothing; of nothing: leave thy idle questions, –
    I am i' th' way to study a long silence,
    To prate were idle, – I remember nothing.
    There's nothing of so infinite vexation   205
    As man's own thoughts.

LODOVICO.   O thou glorious strumpet,
    Could I divide thy breath from this pure air
    When 't leaves thy body, I would suck it up
    And breathe 't upon some dunghill.

VITTORIA.   You, my death's-man;
    Methinks thou dost not look horrid enough,   210
    Thou hast too good a face to be a hangman, –
    If thou be, do thy office in right form;
    Fall down upon thy knees and ask forgiveness.

LODOVICO. O thou hast been a most prodigious comet,
    But I'll cut off your train: – kill the Moor first.   215

VITTORIA. You shall not kill her first. Behold my breast, –
    I will be waited on in death; my servant
    Shall never go before me.

GASPARO. Are you so brave?

VITTORIA.   Yes I shall welcome death
    As princes do some great ambassadors;   220
    I'll meet thy weapon half way.

LODOVICO.   Thou dost tremble, –
    Methinks fear should dissolve thee into air.

VITTORIA. O thou art deceiv'd, I am too true a woman:
    Conceit can never kill me: I'll tell thee what, –
    I will not in my death shed one base tear,   225
    Or if look pale, for want of blood, not fear.

CARLO. Thou art my task, black Fury.

ZANCHE.   I have blood
   As red as either of theirs: wilt drink some?
   'Tis good for the falling sickness: I am proud
   Death cannot alter my complexion,   230
   For I shall ne'er look pale.

LODOVICO.   Strike, strike,
   With a joint motion.

   [*They strike.*]

VITTORIA.   'Twas a manly blow –
   The next thou giv'st, murder some sucking infant,
   And then thou wilt be famous.

FLAMINEO.   O what blade is 't?
   A Toledo, or an English fox?   235
   I ever thought a cutler should distinguish
   The cause of my death, rather than a doctor.
   Search my wound deeper: tent it with the steel
   That made it.

VITTORIA. O my greatest sin lay in my blood.   240
   Now my blood pays for 't.

FLAMINEO.   Th' art a noble sister –
   I love thee now; if woman do breed man
   She ought to teach him manhood: fare thee well.
   Know many glorious women that are fam'd
   For masculine virtue, have been vicious   245
   Only a happier silence did betide them –
   She hath no faults, who hath the art to hide them.

VITTORIA. My soul, like to a ship in a black storm,
   Is driven I know not whither.

FLAMINEO.   Then cast anchor.
   Prosperity doth bewitch men seeming clear,   250
   But seas do laugh, show white, when rocks are near.
   We cease to grieve, cease to be Fortune's slaves,
   Nay cease to die by dying. Art thou gone
   And thou so near the bottom? – false report
   Which says that women vie with the nine Muses   255

For nine tough durable lives: I do not look
Who went before, nor who shall follow me;
No, at myself I will begin and end:
While we look up to heaven we confound
Knowledge with knowledge. O I am in a mist.   260

VITTORIA. O happy they that never saw the court,
Nor ever knew great man but by report.

VITTORIA *dies*.

FLAMINEO. I recover like a spent taper, for a flash
And instantly go out.

Let all that belong to great men remember th' old wives'   265
tradition, to be like the lions i' th' Tower on Candlemas day,
to mourn if the sun shine for fear of the pitiful remainder of
winter to come.

'Tis well yet there's some goodness in my death,
My life was a black charnel: I have caught   270
An everlasting cold. I have lost my voice
Most irrecoverably: farewell glorious villains, –
This busy trade of life appears most vain,
Since rest breeds rest, where all seek pain by pain
Let no harsh flattering bells resound my knell,   275
Strike thunder, and strike loud to my farewell.

Dies.

ENGLISH AMBASSADOR [*within*]. This way, this way; break ope
the doors, this way.

LODOVICO. Ha, are we betray'd? –
Why then let's constantly die all together,
And having finish'd this most noble deed,   280
Defy the worst of fate; not fear to bleed.

Enter AMBASSADORS *and* GIOVANNI [*with* GUARDS].

ENGLISH AMBASSADOR. Keep back the prince, – shoot, shoot, –

[*They shoot, and wound* LODOVICO.]

LODOVICO.   O I am wounded.
I fear I shall be ta'en.

GIOVANNI.   You bloody villains,
   By what authority have you committed
   This massacre?

LODOVICO.   By thine.

GIOVANNI.   Mine?

LODOVICO.   Yes, thy uncle,   285
   Which is a part of thee, enjoin'd us to 't: –
   Thou know'st me I am sure, – I am Count Lodowick, –
   And thy most noble uncle in disguise
   Was last night in thy court.

GIOVANNI.   Ha!

CARLO.   Yes, that Moor
   Thy father chose his pensioner.

GIOVANNI.   He turn'd murderer;   290
   Away with them to prison, and to torture;
   All that have hands in this, shall taste our justice,
   As I hope heaven.

LODOVICO.   I do glory yet,
   That I can call this act mine own: – for my part,
   The rack, the gallows, and the torturing wheel   295
   Shall be but sound sleeps to me, – here's my rest –
   I limb'd this night-piece and it was my best.

GIOVANNI. Remove the bodies, – see my honoured lord,
   What use you ought make of their punishment.
   Let guilty men remember their black deeds   300
   Do lean on crutches, made of slender reeds.

   [*Exeunt.*]

Instead of an epilogue only this of Martial supplies me:

Haec fuerint nobis præmia si placui.

For the action of the play, 'twas generally well, and I dare
affirm, with the joint testimony of some of their own quality,
(for the true imitation of life, without striving to make nature a
monster) the best that ever became them: whereof as I make a
general acknowledgement, so in particular I must remember the
well approved industry of my friend Master Perkins, and confess
the worth of his action did crown both beginning and end.

Finis.

Glossary

adamant – stone of great hardness, identified with the lodestone or magnet

Aesop – writer of fables

affecteth – loves

amain – with full speed

Anacharsis . . . mortar – a Scythian philosopher was put to death in this way by the tyrant Nicocreon, whom he had denounced

ancient – former

anon – soon

apples . . . ashes – the apples of Sodom were beautiful on the outside, but turned to dust

arras – tapestry

arras powder – ground orris root, used by brides to lighten and perfume hair

Artillery Yard – in Bishopsgate, site of target practice

atomies – atoms, tiniest of particles

Attende . . . Brachiano – 'Listen, Lord Brachiano'

ballated – made into a common ballad

bandy factions – group together

Barbary – north-west coast of Africa, with suggestion of 'barbarian'

barriers – tournaments

beaver – face guard of a helmet

bed-staff – stick used in bed-making

bias – weight in the cheek of a bowl

black lake – the Styx, deepest of the rivers of Hades

bowl booty – two players at bowls combined against a third

braches – bitches

breese – gadflies

broke . . . poison'd – the Earl of Leicester was believed to have tried to poison his wife before pushing her to her death down a flight of stairs

broom-men – street cleaners

buckram – coarse starched linen

buttery-hatch – half-door for dispensing drinks

Candlemas – 2 February: a fair day was said to portend harsh weather yet to come

Candy – Candia, i.e., Crete

cantharides – spanish fly, used both medicinally and as a poison

Capuchins – austere branch of Franciscan order of monks

career – short, fast gallop

caroche – coach

carved – here, 'castrated'

casque – helmet, worn for tournaments

cassia – luxurious perfume

Casta est quam nemo rogavit – 'she is chaste whom no one has solicited'

Castle Angelo – in Rome, where the historical Vittoria was held

chamois – soft leather for making undergarments

chaps – jaws

charnel – burial house

cheeks – the side of a bowl, as of a face

Chirurgeon – surgeon

choke-pear – a bitter, unpalatable pear, thus 'hard to swallow'

clapp'd by the heels – put in the stocks

close – secret

closet – private inner room

cloth of tissue – woven from gold thread and silk

codpiece – flap in male breeches

Colossuses – gigantic statues, after the Colossus of Rhodes

come about – turned around

copperas – copper sulphate, fatal in large doses

Concedimus . . . peccatorum – 'we grant you apostolic blessing and remission of sins'

conclavist – servant to the cardinals in the conclave

confederate – allied, conspiratorial

conies – rabbits, also simpletons or women

convertites – reformed prostitutes

Corinth – town in Ancient Greece renowned for both its marble and its prostitutes

corse – corpse

count – a pun on 'cunt'

crusadoes – Portuguese coins marked with a cross

cullis – broth

curtal – horse or dog with docked tail, perhaps a conjurer's familiar

cutler – maker of knives

cypress – delicate material

dead lift – crisis

deadly . . . fart – a Spaniard, Don Diego, was ill-famed for farting in St Paul's Cathedral

decimosexto – very small book

demi-foot-cloth – half-length covering for a horse

Denuntio . . . quartum – 'I bring you joyful news: the most reverend Cardinal Lorenzo de Monticelso has been elected to the Apostolic See and has chosen Paul IV for his name'

devil in crystal – an allusion to the title of the play: to 'behold the devil in crystal' was a proverb meaning 'to be deceived'

dials – i.e., sundials

dispend – exhaust, use up

diversivolent – quarrelsome

dog-days – hottest days of summer, supposedly lustful

dog-fish – cheap fish, also term of abuse

Domine . . . corruptissimam – 'Reverend judge, observe this pestilence, this most corrupt of women'

Domine . . . lævum – 'Lord Brachiano, in battle you were used to the protection of your shield, now you shall hold this up against your infernal enemy.' 'Once you triumphed in battle with your spear; now you shall wield this sacred spear against the enemy of souls.' 'Listen, Lord Brachiano, if you now also approve what has been done between us, turn your head to the right.' 'Be assured, Lord Brachiano, think how many good deeds you have done, and lastly remember that my soul is pledged for yours, if there should be danger.' 'If you now also approve what has been done between us, turn your head to the left'

dottrels – species of plover, easy to hunt: hence, a simpleton

ducats – gold coins widely used in Europe

Dutch doublet – a tight-fitting jacket

ejectment – legal process of eviction from land

electuaries – aphrodisiacs, made of honey or jam

emblem – symbolic picture

engine – tool, instrument

ephemerides – astrological almanac

falling sickness – epilepsy

feathers – plumes, as shed from helmets during a tournament

felly – curved section of wheel

ferret – i.e., ferret out, discover

ferret . . . blowing – blowing in a ferret's face was believed to loosen its hold

fetch a course about – turn tail

figure-flingers – contemptuous term for astrologers

flaw – squall

Flectere . . . movebo – 'If I cannot win the help of the gods above, I shall invoke the lower regions'

fold of lead – i.e., coffin

foot-cloth – cloth hung over the horse of a nobleman

forced – artificial

fore-deeming – prejudging

forswear – renounce on oath

fowler – hunter of game-birds

fowling-piece – light gun for shooting wild fowl

full man – resolute man

fustian – bombastic

gall – bitterness, resentment

gargarism – gargle

geese in the progress – prostitutes following a royal journey

gilder – goldsmith

give credit – believe me

given o'er – abandoned

graduatically – as befits a graduate

grammatical – formal, according to the rules

graz'd – lost in the grass

groats – silver coins of low value

gudgeons – small fish which take any bait: hence, credulous persons

gull – deceive, cheat

Hæc . . . placui – 'these things will be our reward if we have pleased you'

Haec . . . relinques – 'what you leave today will be fed to pigs'

haggard – wild female hawk, hence wanton woman

hams – thighs

happily – haply, perhaps

haunt to 't – frequent it

Homer's frogs – who used bullrushes as pikes

horn-shavings – i.e., as from a cuckold's horns

Ida – Mount Ida, near Troy, where Paris spent his youth as a shepherd

in leon – on a leash

Inopem me copia fecit – 'abundance has left me impoverished'

intelligencers – spies

intelligencing – spying

Irish mantle – plaid worn by Irish peasants

Italian cut-works – open-work embroidery

Jacob's staff – instrument for measuring altitude

jade – bad-tempered horse or woman

juggler – magician, conjurer

Jubilee – a year in which the Church gave indulgences for acts of piety

julio – coin of low value

jump with – run up against, lie with

kennel – gutter

lamprey – eel-like fish

lapwing . . . head - a newly-hatched lapwing was said to run about with its head in the shell

leash – set of three (originally hounds)

lees – sediment, dregs

Lethe – river crossed by the souls of the dead: drinking its waters induced oblivion

leverets – young hares

limb'd – painted

linguist – talker, conversationist

Lucian . . . borse – Lucian in his *Menippos* gave a comic account of the sufferings of the great in purgatory.

Lycurgus – legendary Spartan statesman

mandrake – poisonous and medicinal plant: its root is thought to resemble the human form

manet acta mente repostum – 'it stays undisturbed within my mind'

matachin – sword dance, splendidly costumed and masked

maw – belly

mercer – dealer in luxury goods

moil – mule

moonish – changeable (like the moon)

motion – offer, proposal

mummia – medicine prepared from embalmed flesh

mutton – loose women

Nec . . . molestas – 'you [i.e., this book] need not fear malicious tongues, nor will you be used for wrapping mackerel'

Nemo me impune lacessit – 'no one provokes me with impunity' *nigromancer* – necromancer, conjurer

non . . . dixi – 'you cannot say more against my trifles than I have said myself'

non . . . mori – 'these monuments do not know how to die'

non plus – state of puzzlement

nos . . . nihil – 'we know these things are nothing'

O . . . ilia – 'O strong stomachs of harvesters'

painted comforts – false comforts

panderism – employment as a pander, or pimp

partridge . . . laurel – the partridge was said to purge itself annually by eating laurel leaves

pash'd – smashed

pastry – kitchen

patent – document conferring privilege or licence

patrimony – inheritance from one's father

Perseus – Greek hero who slew the Gorgon

personate – assume the character of

pesthouse – hospital for plague victims

Pew wew – contemptuous expression

philosopher's stone – sought by alchemists, for its property of turning base metal into gold, as also of curing illness

phlegmatic – cold, dull

physic me – make me feel better

pitch'd field – field of battle

plummet – weight on plumbline

ply your convoy – go about your business

politic respect – political motive

Polyphemus – Cyclops, one-eyed giant

poniards – daggers

postern – small door

preferment – promotion

prefix'd – prearranged

pregnant – resourceful, full of ideas

presence – presence chamber, reception room

put off – sell fraudulently

quae negata grata – 'that which is denied is desirable'

quails – small game-birds, thought to feed on poisonous seed

quat – squat

quite – requite, reward

racket away – loss of money at tennis

ranger – game-keeper

Rialto talk – common gossip

rarely – wonderfully

ring-galliard – routine employed in horse-training

rosemary – evergreen herb, emblematic of remembrance

rue – bitter-tasting shrub, emblematic of sorrow

ruffin – slang for 'devil'

Saint Anthony's fire – erysipelas, a disease causing inflammation and reddening of the skin

saffron – the dried stigmas of the Autumnal Crocus, believed to cause merriment, but fatal taken to excess

sallet – salad

Scotch holy bread – bread for the sacrament spread with sheep's liver

screech-owl – barn-owl, thought to be the bearer of bad news

scriveners – scribes, clerks

scruples – tiny pieces

sennet – flourish on the trumpet heralding an entry or procession

service – dishes

shed hairs – i.e., in the course of treatment for venereal disease

signet – official seal

slip them o'er – pass over them

smoor – smother, suffocate

snuff – burnt end of a candle wick

sowing hand – i.e., with sweeping gestures, as sowing seed

Spanish fig – poison, also an indecent gesture

springe – snare, trap

stews – brothels

stibium – antimony, an element used as a poison

stigmatic – deformed

strappado'd – hung up by the hands tied behind the back

suffrage – support

superficies – outward show

Switzers – Swiss mercenaries

taffeta-linings – glossy silk underwear

tagging points – putting points on laces, for fastening clothes

tale of a tub – incredible tale

Tartar – warrior tribe

tendance – care

tent – probe

Thessaly – region of Greece associated with poisonous herbs and witchcraft

tilter – one who takes part in a tilt, or joust

tilting – jousting, also 'copulating'

Toledo . . . fox – kinds of swords

tows'd – handled roughly or indelicately

traverse – curtain

tumultuary – hasty, haphazard

turn in post – return speedily

unction – ointment, as in 'extreme unction', for the dying

under the line – at the equator

use – usury, interest

uttered – offered for sale

valance – bed hangings

ventages – finger-holes (in wind instruments)

verge – boundary of royal jurisdiction

viands – provisions

voided out – emptied out, dug up

walnut tree – proverbially said, like a woman or an ass, to bear more fruit for being beaten

wild ducks – here, prostitutes

willow – emblematic of mourning and spurned love

without book – from memory

wolf – ulcer, growth

Wolner – notorious Elizabethan glutton who died eating a raw eel

woman-keeper – female nurse

wound up – i.e., in his shroud

yew-tree – associated with death and grief